Rick & Cheryl

Leave your Imprint

Kerry Mensch

LEAVING YOUR
LIFE
IMPRINT

To my mother, Melonee, and Pa Paw Nichols

LEAVING YOUR

LIFE
IMPRINT

A Legacy Story that Lives Beyond One's Lifetime

KENNY MAUCK

Copyright © 2019 by Kenny Mauck

Leaving Your Life Imprint:
A Legacy Story that Lives Beyond One's Lifetime

All rights reserved. No part of this publication may be reproduced, distributed, or transmitted in any form or by any means, including photocopying, recording, or other electronic or mechanical methods, without the prior written permission of the publisher, except in the case of brief quotations embodied in critical reviews and certain other noncommercial uses permitted by copyright law.

Quantity sales special discounts are available on quantity purchases by corporations, associations, and others. For details, contact the publisher at the address above.

Manufactured and printed in the United States of America.
Distributed globally by Boss Publishing.

New York | Los Angeles | London | Sydney

ISBN:
Hard cover 978-1-949873-35-1

Contents

INTRODUCTION			1
ACKNOWLEDGEMENTS			15
CHAPTER 1	Passages		19
CHAPTER 2	Uncharted Waters		33
CHAPTER 3	Facing the Headwinds		53
CHAPTER 4	Batten Down the Hatches		77
CHAPTER 5	Wade in the Water		91
CHAPTER 6	Course Corrections		109
CHAPTER 7	Finding Your Sea Legs		127
CHAPTER 8	Discovery		169
CHAPTER 9	Assembling Your Crew		195
CHAPTER 10	The Admirals Club		213
CHAPTER 11	Captain's Log		235
CHAPTER 12	The Wind in Your Sails		253
ABOUT THE AUTHOR: KENNY MAUCK			269
CONTACT INFORMATION			271

Introduction

HAVING JUST PENNED *my last sentence of this book, I sit slowly sipping my hot tea. This coupled with the sun rising quickly has created some appreciated warmth on this brisk morning. My faithful sidekick, Manny our Miniature Pincher, lays snuggled and curled next to me, snoring lightly. This ritual of ours began some twenty-four months ago.*

God has provided the pond behind our home and wild game as an amazing inspiration and backdrop for me to write. As I look up, a doe has walked down to the pond from behind the trees to the water's edge. She seems mesmerized by viewing herself in the clear glassy water. Like this doe, I find myself in a season of reflection, the prime of my life, a time of seeking what really matters, and just as importantly, what really doesn't.

When I started researching my family, I did not intend to write a book. I was simply inquiring to find some basic information about my family – dates of birth, locations, ports of entry, and death certificates. Yet as I have worked my way through my ancestry, I began to pull away from the research. I started experiencing some anxiety with troubling thoughts and questions about my own mortality.

One night, it got so bad that I was suddenly awakened from a deep sleep by anxious thoughts accompanied by heavy breathing and sweating. I quickly sat up, planting my feet down on the floor to make sure I was still alive. This overwhelming thought caused me to frightfully ponder these words, "One day, this heart of mine will no longer beat, and this body will breath its last breath. My whole life is passing right before my eyes so quickly."

Initially I asked myself, "Is this just me?" But thankfully, one restless evening I recalled Psalm 90:12–17, whereby God began speaking through the Psalmist David. He reassured me by branding these inspired words onto my heart, "Teach us to number our days."

I realized at that moment, God wasn't responding just to David or myself. This message was for us all – friends, family members, and anyone else willing to intentionally embrace, cherish, and fully take in each day of one's life.

Even during times of celebration over the last fourteen months, I have lost some of my closest family and friends: my first-cousin Landy near Thanksgiving, our dear friend's daughter Kristi on New Year's, my father-in-law Ernie on my birthday, and on Christmas, my Aunt Marciel. Life is truly a gift and needs to be lived with purpose. A dear friend of ours numbers his days by beginning each prayer with, "Lord, thank you for the gift of life."

As this book has progressed, more profound questions have risen within me about how we now connect with each other daily in this modern electronic age. Have our meaningful interactions now given way to texting and changed how we communicate with our dear friends and loved ones? We seem to now be totally enraptured by social media and touch screens. Our world is fully accessed by a simple touch of our finger that involves less human interaction yet one that does our banking, grocery shopping, movies, etc.

Could these wonderful things of convenience also create the unintended consequence of us moving further away from each other, preferring instead to text than to speak? Are we losing those special places of time to express our love, to make amends, or to simply laugh and cry with one another? Why do we wait until death to even consider sharing life's applicable stories with our children?

Three Epiphany Moments that Inspired Me To Write *Leaving Your Life Imprint*

The first epiphany that steered me to ultimately write this book started in January 2014, as a doctoral student at Trevecca University. I was assigned to read a New York Times *best seller by Professor Randy Paushe of Carnegie Mellon, entitled* The Last Lecture. *Randy's doctor had given him an end-of-life notice due to an aggressive cancer. So with little time left, he decided to do a video and write his memoir. His wife wanted him to concentrate primarily on their children his final year.*

Randy chose writing the book instead, thinking his children would be too young to remember him. He lamented in the latter chapters of his book, "Why didn't I take the time when I had it to write my story"

The seconds, minutes, hours, and days spent on the book was meant to give to his family something to remember him by, but unfortunately, was competing with what little time he had left with them. This amazing insight that Randy gave to people like me was simple: if you have a life story, don't wait until the end of life to begin sharing it.

The next epiphany moment came on November 14, 2014, when invited to participate in Christ Church's sixtieth anniversary service in Nashville, Tennessee. I was asked to share about LifeCare, our legacy faith-based nonprofit company founded while attending and serving on staff at the church. (At that time, Christ Church was only one of the few Nashville mega churches.) The church was founded by one of the kindest, most loving, humblest, and most caring men I have ever known, Pastor L. H. Hardwick.

Before sharing about LifeCare, I briefly spoke as to Pastor Hardwick's own legacy story. I have come to realize, one should never give one's legacy story without first giving preference and acknowledgement to the one who inspired and imprinted your own.

So, I began by describing Pastor Hardwick's humble beginnings, like marrying his first wife Montelle on Christmas Eve, December 24, 1950, when she was nineteen, and he was eighteen. (Ironically, Pastor's Hardwick's second wife, Carol, was Montelle's dear friend and thus the only one Montelle had given approval should he ever remarry).

Pastor Hardwick began preaching at the age of eighteen, and his joyful and humorous wife helped him start a little church on the corner of Rose and Sadler. I had interviewed Mike and Steve, Pastor Hardwick's sons and both significant to the church's success, in a podcast last year. Mike stated with a chuckle, "Two of these four families were our own family. My mom's parents and our family were half of the church's total members."

For years, Pastor Hardwick never had enough for a salary, so he worked as a chaplain at the state prison and taught his boys how to get up early and help him sell Krispy Kreme donuts, box lunches, and dinners as ways of helping support the church. Funds were needed to run the buses for children and families in need of a ride or for various other needs of the church.

Mike and Steve remember their dad cutting grass on hot days in his suit. Why? Some days there wasn't much time between a funeral or a hospital call. These legacy blocks were carefully laid and became part of the Christ Church legacy too. After years of working and volunteering for the church, eventually Pastor Hardwick was given a small salary.

Looking out over the large crowd attending that morning, I jokingly shared from the platform that as a counselor, the odds of him marrying at the age of eighteen and remaining a pastor at one location for fifty years was slim to none. We all had a good laugh until I asked everyone to please stand and give honor and thanks to this great faithful servant of God after all these years.

As the congregation gave him the great standing ovation he so rightly deserved, I felt inadequate to even be part of this service. Why? I remember *watching him talking in his office, sitting next to the great Billy Graham. Pastor humbly put Reverend Graham in his own chair and got him something to drink. This gracious man of Finley, Tennessee, had not only left an imprint on my life but the lives of hundreds of great pastors he had met along the way.*

A plaque was given in honor of this anniversary of the church earlier to both Pastor Hardwick and the church's current pastor, Reverend Dan Scott, by our LifeCare board. However, the highlight was a specific sermon on the video that revealed the inspiration of me starting our nonprofit company.

It started with a sermon by Pastor Hardwick entitled, BHAG ("Big Hairy Audacious Goal"). It was a message of confirmation I needed that prompted me to realize God was actually calling me to reach out beyond our local church and community for Christ.

This sermon reminded me that now was the time to fulfill the promise I had made to a little nine-year-old African-American child named "Carlos" in 1992, when I was his therapist. I had tucked this promise down deep inside my heart due to the enormity of what it would take to fulfill it. In fact, it would take a miracle to fulfill a goal such as this.

Little did I realize some twenty-two-plus years later that God would do just that. He kept His end of the commitment as evidenced by the thousands upon thousands of children and families helped over the years. This 2014 celebratory service would prove pivotal and another motivation to write this imprinted story.

Looking at Obstacles as Opportunities!

Had it not been for Pastor Hardwick, his two sons Mike and Steve, the teachings of Dave Ramsey on finances, Dan Miller explaining the importance of a mission statement, my cousin Mike helping with policies, and my first cousin Landy giving me a thirty-day loan to meet payroll, our legacy company, LifeCare, would most likely never have happened.

Fortunately, I also had a dad, father-in-law, and dear friends serving on my board to help fill in the gaps during those early foundational years.

Winston Churchill once stated, "One should look at obstacles as opportunities, not problems."

Still, how does one build a new company, realizing you have limited management skills necessary to run it? For example, I had no business degree. limited resources, and no staff. Well, as you journey with me through this story, you will see how God's favor and mercy were prevalent every step of the way.

Looking back, I realize now after employing many hundreds of employees and managing millions of dollars, it had to be God's favor that allowed us to serve thousands upon thousands of our state's most poor, vulnerable, neglected, and abused children, as well as those with rehabilitative, physical, and special exceptional supports. This book will help show you how after twenty-two years and building two nonprofits, God still can and will make the impossible, possible despite inabilities like mine.

Completing Our Will — The Final Epiphany Moment in Writing the Book

At the beginning of 2015, after some prodding from one of my fellow friends, my wife Raye Ann and I decided to have an attorney draw up a will for us. The attorney ensured that we divided up our investments, buildings, land, and other assets to our children equally.

When it was completed, I left with some initial peace, finally knowing it was fully done, and our children would be fine. This sense of peace ironically would be short-lived in that on the drive home, I felt something was still missing. Surely, there had to be something more meaningful to give to my kids and grandkids.

I kept mulling these things over in my mind, yet I still did not want Raye Ann to think I wasn't happy with the will. As the months continued, it kept bothering me that I wasn't giving something of real substance to my children about my life or that of their ancestors.

So, around the early part of 2015, ancestry.com popped up on my screen at work, and I began to ask myself, "How can I share a story with my kids about their heritage and that of their descendants if I haven't even taken the time to find out about my own ancestors?"

A few days later, I got up and made the decision that it was time I commit to doing some real significant research about my family's heritage. I had been told my family was of German descent, but I had no idea if this was folklore or fact. No matter what, I was committed now to find out.

I became inundated with a multitude of questions. Where did my family come from? Who was the first person in our family to come to America? Why did they come here?

My search and journey for meaning had begun. Over the next two and a half years, I began my new routine early in the morning to write or do research and continue to give Manny his uninvited snuggle space. I began by searching diligently online and in libraries to find various family historical sites and books and to seek permission to enter their own family trees. However, the ancestry.com site and outreach to my immediate and extended family, including that of my parents, evolved into hundreds of questions and became an everyday event.

My Admitted Addiction

As time went on, I got up early, went to bed late, drove my wife and kids crazy, asking them to turn down the tube and keep my dinner on the stove. I soon realized my original intention of just charting births, deaths, and who begat who was not enough. So began the next level.

Within nine months, I was now in the deep guts of research and was beginning to form some of my ancestors' stories. I was like a little kid discovering hidden treasures in a candy store. For years, I had done family trees as a therapist, but this one was of significant interest. Not only was it my own flesh and blood I was finding out about, but I was making a connection between family members and the generations to which they were linked.

As I began threading the stories as far back as the early 1700s, it was as if I was watching an old black-and-white reel-to-reel projector, watching real pictures, and matching faces and stories. A storyline was forming together, no longer a bunch of disjointed accounts but people and stories that were intimate, funny, sad, full of loss, and joy, one that was becoming part of my own extended story I never knew existed. I started bringing tissues, and Manny tried to stop the tears. I found myself smiling, laughing, hurt, and frustrated. Most importantly, it was all coming to life now. My family story was starting to make sense. Now instead of the fear of not knowing, feelings of hope were forming as more unearthed treasures surfaced. I strongly empathized with some of these real-to-life stories that would stretch from me, my father, and every grandfather up the chain, all the way up to my sixth great-grandfather.

I found out our family truly did come from Germany and in what town they lived. Eventually, the names of Hans, Frederick, Samuel, Joseph, William, and Tom were no longer just distant relatives; they had become part of my own heart. The good, the bad, the ugly, and the beautiful parts of my family's story were no longer hidden away in layers of words and pictures with no connections. Each one of my grandfathers was suddenly alive and now in a full panoramic view.

I also recognized my family had to develop diverse friends with diverse experiences and backgrounds. Some of my relatives you will read about experienced significant stories of risk, exploration, marital issues, and loss. Some were faithful to each other, and some were not.

All these characters were not only flesh and blood, but I realized they were also all relatable to those of my own friends, therapist, administrators, business CEOs, blue-collars workers, my colleagues, co-leaders, coaches, artist, educators, and minister friends.

Our Trip to Germany...

Prior to beginning chapter one, I wanted to conclude this introduction by briefly sharing a recent trip to Germany that my wife and I took. I hope as you read, you will see how these last few pages set up the entire book. I hope it will create that sense of inspiration with you as it did with me. The trip was amazing and touched the very soul of me.

GERMANY — Going Back to My Homeland

On September 13, 2018, Raye Ann and I travelled to London, England, on an overnight eight-and-half-hour fight from Nashville. After a several-hour layover, we flew onto Frankfurt, Germany. We would be celebrating our thirty-fifth anniversary primarily in Italy, but we had scheduled three days in Giessen, Germany, some fifty-five miles northeast of Frankfurt. It was here where our Mauck (Mock) family and imprinted story began. This was the place where Hans Peter Mauck, my sixth-generational great-grandfather, was born in 1707. His Lutheran parents were Wilhelm and Sophia Mauk.. (The spelling of Mock, Mauk, and Mauck evolved over time. The German and English phonetics caused translation problems in regards to spelling, intonation, and blends.)

During our one-hour flight from London to Germany, we flew over the English Channel. I had just figured out how many miles we would have traveled internationally, over 4,571 miles to get here.

It would have taken me approximately nine hours in total from Nashville to Frankfurt and close to another hour to get to Giessen, ten hours in total, whereas in comparison, it took sixth-generational great-grandfather, Hans Peter Mauck, a total of approximately 150 days, or nearly 4,000 hours to get from Giessen, Germany to Philadelphia, Pennsylvania, in 1733. To think it took me less than half a day to get there in comparison to a twenty-five-year-old coming on an English passenger boat was overwhelming to me.

Soon, I would be attempting to trace the actual steps of Hans Peter. Everything was suddenly very surreal. Upon driving to Giessen, I realized I was on the autobahn. Cars passed me at some 140 miles per hour. Things like this, Hans would have never imagined in the 1700s, but the temptation to speed was too appealing. One hundred twenty miles per hour in the slow lane for a few minutes was very enlightening.

We checked into our small bed and breakfast, a large older home. The keeper of the home spoke limited to almost-no English.

Not knowing any German, I quickly saw the immediate barrier Hans would have first encountered. It must have taken him six months, maybe even years to learn a language about which he and our ancestral family knew nothing.

Our German meals were very different, yet in the city, there was some American food. Speaking with the folks in Giessen, a common lunch or dinner would include sausage, rice, homemade cheeses, tomatoes, and cucumbers. Breakfast could consist of cereal, eggs, yogurt, meat, potatoes, or oats.

One thing I also learned in Germany was that there was little to no ice. They believed in serving you drinks from glass bottles, no ice, no plastic cups, forks, spoons, or knives. It was nothing but real silverware, plates, and glasses. Any less was considered offensive.

Making a meal was the time to converse and meant to be special. Life seemed simple despite the modern changes in this little city that had once been a village. Hans and our Mauk family worked very hard as farmers, but as many Lutherans, our family was treated like dogs beneath the table. This was due to wealthy kings and landlords, who without concern of law or sense of justice, bought off religious leaders to look the other way as Lutherans lost their properties.

First and Second Full Day in Giessen...

The first day, we relaxed from our long flight. The next day, we met the local Lutheran lady pastor of Giessen, who though knowledgeable about her Lutheran church, could not determine which church Hans and his family attended.

She shared on the map where Hans would have likely departed from the local river due to where it intersected north and south from the roads at that time. The west side of the river would lead them eventually down river to the Rhine.

Last Day in Germany, September 15, 2018

Our last day in Germany was the most rewarding. The city downtown indicated where our Mauk family would have shopped for goods as farmers. The beautiful town square with Bavarian-looking shudders and cobblestone streets were clean. Some of the town had to be reconstructed after World War II. Surely this little village was a quaint place now, but at a one point, it was an eyesore due to the ravages of war and death that incurred.

The most rewarding and emotionally fulfilling experience was locating the Lahn River whereby my sixth great-grandfather, Hans Peter Mauck, would place his little family canoe and start down the tributary to the large English passenger ship named Samuel. This ship would have been waiting for all of its passengers to board on the Rhine River sometime in the late spring of 1733, to ultimately head to America.

As Raye and I followed the map, sure enough, it showed this was where the railroad and roads intersected near the waterway downtown as the pastor had told us. As we came underneath the railroad tracks in a small tunnel, my eyes suddenly gushed with unexpected tears. There in front of me was the quaint tributary where Hans would have left. A beautiful walkway was next to the river. It was here where I knew why I had to come some 4,500 miles away from home.

The river was extremely serene with kayakers rowing in unison. Prior to leaving, we ate at a nice German-Italian restaurant next to the Lahn River.

I was captivated by it all and whispered to my wife as a couple passed by us, "Raye, it's overwhelming, isn't it?"

"Yes," she whispered back, "it is."

I continued. "I want you to know the tears you see from my eyes are not about me or for me; they are for him. His parents had saved most of their entire life for the one and only ticket to America for their son, and he was a young man eight years younger than our own son."

Everything he had ever known in his life, he would now be paddling away from, his home, friends, and pastor. Hans Peter Mauck made the brave decision in the spring of 1733 to travel to America, although he must have shed many tears. He ultimately made the trip to honor his parents' wishes. His family had been persecuted for their faith. He wanted to keep their and his hopes alive in an effort to find a place where he could freely worship without torture or fear of having his land taken.

To avoid being seen by those oppressing the Lutherans, he had to have travelled by the moon shining on the water at night and hid in the cove as needed during the day. As he traveled down this long tributary, he had to eventually connect with the much larger Rhine River, where the Samuel waited.

When he said goodbye to his parents, they and he knew it would be the last time they would ever set eyes on each other again. The parting must have been the toughest thing he had ever been asked to do.

Little did he know what would soon be facing him!

It would take Hans Peter Mauck (Mock) over five months to get from Giessen, Germany to Philadelphia, Pennsylvania. The very spot I was standing seemed like a sacred place. It was here where our Hans determined if our name, our faith, and our way of life would continue, die, or turn around and go back to where our family suffered under an evil tyrant named Hitler some 200 years later.

Before I left the beautiful landing on the Lahn River, I captured this place with my camera to keep it as an imprint in which to share with my family, signifying this as the very place my twenty-five-year-old sixth-time grandfather would last see his home and family. I realized that while standing on that very spot, few, if any, of my relatives would have this opportunity. I could only tell my dad since most of our family had passed away.

Hans hoped to make it to America. He would never know that some 285 years later, I would come and visit him. On behalf of all the Maucks living in America, I would honor his decision of risking it all by journeying to America.

(As you travel onward through this book based on a true-life story, an application section at the end of each chapter has been created so that you can begin developing your own legacy story and those of your own children, friends, and loved ones.)

Acknowledgements

I WANT TO FIRST THANK MY WIFE, Raye Ann for your love and endurance over the last thirty-five years in marrying a dreamer, entrepreneur, nonprofit CEO, songwriter, risk-taker, and now after thirty-six months, an author. Writing *Leaving your Life Imprint* has been an amazing journey. I also want to thank God for gifting me as a father with six awesome imprints, our adult children Landon, Megan, and Kelsey, and our three grandchildren, "Awesome Easton," "Super Cooper," and "Princess Gracelyn Hope." I believe our six-time German great-grandfather, Hans Peter Mauck, would be proud!

I also want to thank my parents, Louie and Melonee Mauck, married sixty-four years now, as well as my big sister Candy, a rock in my life and someone with whom I share cherished memories to this day. Also, my brother-in-law, Brad, someone I consider closer than any brother, and their sons, my two buffed police-officer nephews, Nic and Ryan, and their families. Lastly, my sister Tammy and her two girls, Vickie and Vivian, as well as my mother-in-law, Ann Robertson, and Brent and Dina Robertson.

Pastor L.H. Hardwick, my deepest appreciation for you allowing me the opportunity to direct our counseling services at Christ Church and for reminding me in a famous sermon to keep my promises. Also, for you leading your two sons, Mike and Steve, who taught me by their example and support, what skills are needed to lead.

Then, there are four amazing people to thank in completing this book. First Michelle Borquez, the one who has been my greatest encourager throughout the entire process, her other great BOSS Publishing staff, like Diana and Michael. Then there's Alison Stevens, who took my raw story and worked with me to help bring certain areas alive, helping rewrite areas that needed it, a process that included brutal honesty, candidness, laughter, joyful tears, and a realization that at the end, through our synergy, God was creating a legacy story to help change lives for the better, not just by reading it, but experiencing it by the applications provided.

But one of the most wonderful blessings was having *Ken Abraham, an eighteen-New York Times best-selling author, help guide us throughout critical stages of writing this imprint that is based on a true-life story and the characters within my Mauck/Nichols ancestry family heritage.* More importantly, I am honored that Ken and his wife Lisa have become such dear friends of ours over the years. Then there's my friend *Dave Ramsey,* my fellow Eagle (a band of brothers and group influencers he initiated), who has helped promote the launching of our book by allowing use of his nationally syndicated radio station, interviewing via podcast the *likes of Attorney General, Alberto Gonzalez, Dr. Tim Clinton, Movie Score Producer, Reverend L. H. Hardwick and sons, Reverend Dan Scott, Deneen Turner, and others.*

I would be remiss if I didn't also thank my biggest influencers and mentors in my life as well, such as Don Evans and my Business and Life Coach Bill Campbell, Coach Don Marsh, another life mentor and high school track coach, Tennessee House Representative Mark White, Bill and Stacey Spencer, Erick Strickland,

Rob Mortensen, the Honorable Judge Steve Hornsby, Dave and Bernice Matejcek, George Lee Glass and family, Reverend Chuck and Jamie Lawrence, the Pulley family, and friends from Christ Temple in Huntington.

Thank you to my lifelong friends from childhood through college, Greg and Tom Gardner, Pat and Kim Campbell, Kerri Powell, and Ken and Stacie Tucker.

I would like to thank those who helped me start and/or have remained faithful as leaders with LifeCare all these years in leadership: Sean McPherson, Jim Carter, David Thomas, Rebecca Rahman, Christal Wise, Myrna Kemp, James Davis, and Tory Woodard. Also, Marion Killion, Dominque Miller, and Ken Graham served as part of our initial counseling staff on the in-home staff.

I want give special mention as to one of the best therapist I have ever had the opportunity to work with, a wonderful Christian named Mignonne Sawyer, one who specialized in caring for women's issues, depression, and multiple-personality disorders. She and her lovely family will forever be special to me. Mignonne's standard of excellence left an imprint on Christ Church and Lifecare, something our Clinical Director Dr. Dave Thomas continues to this day.

I want to thank LifeCare past and present Board of Directors, Eagles, and LifeCare Heritage and Foundations, Bill Campbell, Don Evans, Dan Finley, Bruce Boder, Jeff Parish, Eddy Richey, Ron Doyle, Dan and Jo Ann Miller, Dan Scott, and advisor to the board, Dave Ramsey.

*In memory and gratitude, board members Ernest Robertson, Landy Gardner, and Dave Cavender.

With appreciation, I want to thank Eagle influencers, Gene Riley, Don Scurlock, Jeff Mosely, David George, Aaron Walker, and Tom Summers.

Thank you to my cousins, Mike and Brenda Berner, Rebecca Foster, Ronnie and Lanora Foster, Lauren Cantu, Mark and Tammie Foster, Joy Gardner, Lauren Hodge, Dionne Dismuke, as well as Ken, Jeff Johnson, and extended Mauck family way too long to list.

I want to thank my good friend, Craig Campbell, for assisting as consultant support in terms of any potential larger venues or cross-over appeal as to the importance of one's story.

Lastly, but most importantly, I want to thank my Lord and Savior, Jesus Christ, for without a doubt, He is the ultimate and eternal imprint on my life, the "Keeper of our redemptive story," one that will live beyond our lifetime.

* * * * *

As for those who have also been our dear friends who may have not been directly related to the book or LifeCare and yet have significance in our life, please note the five stars attached as the recognized symbol of your life imprint on us.

CHAPTER 1

Passages

> "What can we gain by sailing to the moon if we are not able to cross the abyss that separates us from ourselves? This is the most important of all voyages of discovery, and without it, all the rest are not only useless, but disastrous."
>
> — THOMAS MERTON

AS I AM STANDING ON MY BACK DECK, a large crane dives perfectly over the pond, spearing a fish within seconds. I watch with fascination as he skims beautifully over the water before landing effortlessly with his prize breakfast near the far bank.

Our backyard is the best place I have found for inspiration to study and write. Early in the morning or late in the afternoon, the flora and fauna that surround my home provide a spectacular creative backdrop.

Here, in this beautiful setting primed for reflection and introspection, is where I have realized the importance of story. What started as the simple desire to document our family history, including the migration of our German ancestors to America in the 1700s, has become my life-changing, eye-opening journey. The most impactful was the information I uncovered about the life of my sixth great-grandfather, Peter Hans Mauck, and his voyage to America in 1733.

Hans Peter Mauck 1707–1771
(My Sixth Generational Grandfather)

I can only imagine that at only twenty-five years old, Hans was probably both scared and excited as he embarked on the ship called the *Samuel* in the spring of 1733 with 291 passengers, including the captain, Hugh Percy. He was in good company with most of his traveling companions consisting mostly of Lutheran families and couples with dreams and aspirations that come with traveling to a new land.

The passenger ship wasn't large by today's standards, especially with so many travelers aboard, measuring a mere 140-feet by 30-feet by 15-feet. Even the cramped six-feet by two-feet individual sleeping quarters that were housed three floors below deck wouldn't deter them.

As a result, each of those travelers acquired their own story, including my ancestor, Hans. As I dug deeper into his story, I felt like I was unwrapping a gift that led me to a missing key piece of the treasure map of my life. Here is his story through his journal as I imagined it:

July 3: These days are beginning to run together. It is difficult to tell one from another. Can this be over a month and a half that has passed? It does not seem that long. But I count 45 days. All ordinary, and sailing has been unhindered for the most part, except for occasional rain that quickly passes. Dark, even ominous clouds were on the horizon this morning, however, but our Captain Percy seemed unconcerned.

My new friend, an older grandfatherly type by the name of Thomas, and I had a game of cards on deck and talked of his dreams of owning a tavern in the new world. Thomas looks like he could be one of the rough sailors onboard. I sense secrets lurking beneath the surface, more like something he is running from than the new life so many here sprint toward. The winds picked up considerably into the evening today, more so than any other day thus far, so we have returned from the above deck to our quarters for the night.

July 4: The wind is stronger, and the waves have gained strength. Captain Percy and our first mate met at the bow of the ship this morning, away from the eyes and ears of passengers. I saw the concern as they observed the dark clouds that appear to have gained on our position overnight. I fear we are losing ground to the approaching storm as the waves and wind continue to intensify. Even catching a westerly wind for a good part of the day has not pushed us out of reach. Our Lutheran leaders prayed within the safety of our quarters this evening in lieu of on deck as is the norm.

July 5: Captain Percy and the crew have been fully engaged with the storm today, as it has all but overtaken us. Thomas and I snuck atop deck to a sheltered spot out of the way. Captain Percy shouted many orders as the crew quickly obeyed, tying down loose sails, repairing damaged lines, and scrambling to secure all doors and windows as the captain kept an eye on the horizon through his telescope. The captain then met with his crew briefly, the contents of the meeting I could not ascertain, but my fears were confirmed when he went below deck to meet with the leadership.

Thomas and I followed down a different set of stairs to hear the captain's warnings and instructions for us passengers. Every man will be required for us to survive. The pounding rain grows louder as if it will bore right through the hull. The winds drive us over the waves as if to thrust us over the edge and plunge us to the ocean floor. I cannot sleep for the roughness and the fearful cries of the elderly and children. I still hear the crew above us on deck, attempting to keep us on course.

July 6: Few slept last night. Even with sunlight trying to break through the storm, we are still tossed about and must secure everything we can in our quarters. The captain's eyes did not match his attempts to encourage us that the ship is holding up. All the men, including myself, were led to the deck to assist the crew with removing debris and makeshift repairs in an attempt to avoid further damage to the ship. I could not believe my eyes or that we survived the night. We are all meeting to pray that God would help us. The storm continues, and the seas are not done with us yet.

July 8: Thomas and I have spent the last two days bailing out water with buckets. The storm still rages. Evenings are the worst. The children cry, and parents were unable to console or quiet them. Sleep evades us all.

July 9: Day 4 of the storm, and Day 3 of the women, children, and elderly trapped below deck to avoid the danger outside. Sickness and anxiety are settling in; all are desperate for sun and something other than the putrid air we are imprisoned with.

July 11: Tragedy came upon us today. My heart grieves over the death of children from illness. God, I do not understand. Another child lost at sea, swept off by waves breaking over the bow as he escaped the hold of his mother and father trying to gasp for fresh air. The door was open only for a moment, and he was gone. Pneumonia and food poisoning plague our elderly. I cannot sleep for the wails of mourning parents tonight.

July 13: The storm violently tossed me from my bed in the dark of the morning. The gale has regained strength, snapping masts and slamming them to the deck, killing one of our crew. No one, not even myself or Thomas, is permitted above deck. Waves send water down the stairwells to our quarters below, and we cannot keep up with the bailing. Our ship creaks as if it is breaking in two. Thunder shakes the hull. Frightened children scream throughout the night. The women pray loudly and continually. There will be no sleep tonight.

July 15: Morning. The waves are overrunning our ship. The storm is winning this fight. Captain Percy has instructed us to keep items that float within reach should he order an abandon ship. With the loss of our masts and severe damage, we are lifeless and at the mercy of the storm. Some have prayed. Most labor tirelessly to return as much of the sea's water to it as possible. I cannot eat, as I have been throwing up for two days. Although my faith is still strong, I am prepared to leave this earth. All of us are at our end physically and mentally. So tired.

Evening. I am hungry and thirsty but still cannot drink nor keep solid food down. We continue to take shifts, bailing water without pause. Exhaustion is my constant companion. I have finished the letter to Mama and Papa and sealed it inside a whiskey bottle no doubt left by a drunken shipmate. For 12 days, torrential rains and winds have given us no reprieve. Even now, the ship rises and falls, creaking and moaning, an unfortunate constant motion fed by the strong gale winds and seas. It's as if a monster has arisen from the depths of the ocean, relentlessly battering us over and over again. Even though my faith and hope have not yet failed me, my body and mind have nothing left. So, I pen these last remaining notes in my diary to record the dire circumstances we now face and will heave the bottled letter toward Germany in hopes it gets to my parents. I fear the storm and waves are overtaking us and that we will not make it through the night.

> (To whoever may find this letter, most likely found after my death at sea on the *Samuel*, please see this letter is delivered to my parents, Mr. Jonan Wilhelm and Sofia Elizabeth, of the Village of Gieben, Germany, near the Lahn River.)
>
> Dear Papa and Mama,
>
> I write this letter to you as I believe my time is short. Our ship has become disabled due to damage caused by violent storms, and I fear these moments may be my last.

Mama, Papa, do not let sorrow overtake you. Instead, focus on the good memories. My life as your only son leaves me with nothing but the greatest affection for you. I have no regrets, nor should you. Your selfless, sacrificial gift of sending me to a better life in the New World is a testament of your love for me, and I am forever grateful.

Mama, you prayed the night before I left for an angel to accompany me on my journey at sea. That prayer has been such a warm blanket to my soul! I was hesitant to come to America because I didn't want to leave you behind, but you both insisted I take the money you have worked so hard to save, enough for one passage, and go. You saved me from a life of war and oppression like that of my friends. You wanted more for me than a life of shame and ridicule that our Lutheran faith brings. Be proud, as I am, at the risk we all have taken, seeking a new homeland where I can openly confess that Jesus Christ is our high priest and the only one who can pay for our sins.

I prayed as well that night, asking God for peace and favor if I was to go the next morning. He answered, giving me complete peace as I came downstairs and shared our last meal as a family together. I wish I could have been stronger for you when it was time to say goodbye, Papa. But hearing you and Mama weep over me, the memories of my years in Germany, my friends, and you as my parents flooded my mind. It was too overwhelming, and I could not hold back my tears. If I don't make it to America, please know I did my best. I hope to build a life for my own family as you and Mama did for me and to carry on the Mauck name.

If it is God's will that I awaken in heaven, I will await both of you at the gates. To live will take a miracle sent from God above. If He chooses to send one, I will continue to make you proud. It is in His hands now!

I love you.

Your dearest son,
Hans

July 19: *I woke yesterday from what seemed like a horrible dream to people all around me. George and his wife Mary sat with me and gave me a small glass of water, saying they have been caring for me. I have been delirious with food poisoning and only able to consume small amounts of water. I have no memory of it. I wondered for a moment if I was still dreaming and if I was truly alive. Since waking, I have been able to keep down a spoonful of beans and barley. Sun shone through the open door at the top of the stairs. I asked how long I had been sleeping. Three days.*

July 20: *Today, I am well enough to walk on the deck with assistance. I am still not strong, but I am glad for the breeze that breathes new life into my being. Most of the masts that had been snapped by the storm are repaired. The Samuel is on its way again as the sails flap beautifully in concert with the wind. Sea air has replaced the stale and horrible smells associated with 12 days of being isolated below the main deck of the boat.*

As I rounded the stern on my slow assisted walk, I realized I am not dead. I AM NOT DEAD. I shouted, "I AM ALIVE!" I startled a baby who began to cry. What a beautiful sound.

July 21: *All is well with the exception of Thomas, my friend. I inquired today of his whereabouts, but no one knows. No one knows who he is. George and Mary have said they only took care of me but did hear me mention his name as I talked in my sleep. But there is no Thomas on this ship. I am at a loss for an explanation.*

August 1: *I feel I have healed completely. I have been visiting the sick and weak below deck, helping where I can. The captain was glad to see me up and about again. There have been seven deaths, four adults and three children, from food poisoning as a result of contamination from the salt water coming onboard. Even so, today was a special day. A baby was born. Something to rejoice in, and I see it in the faces of my fellow passengers. We are thankful to be alive and share in new life.*

August 17: The captain has told us we are just hours from entering the harbor of Philadelphia. Upon hearing this, I stood at the bow of the boat, arms lifted toward heaven, thanking God for His mercies. I did not try to hide the tears that freely flowed as I thought of Mama and Papa. Even now, I cannot hold them back. My parents' dream of their only son living in America will come true. My hope of carrying on the family name lives! No longer will I live under persecution for my faith.

May these written words ever remind me of the sacrifices made for this new life for myself and for generations that follow. I live to serve my God, to make my parents proud. May God help me make my life count for something greater than just myself.

My Story

Here I sit impacted by a man who is generations disconnected from me, and yet we are so connected. Our choices, our journeys, our stories, our legacies unfold before me like a beautiful tapestry. Hans' story is woven with excitement, adventure, and harrowing experiences, all leading to a new life of freedom. Mine reads a little differently.

My story includes a promise made to a little boy and a catalyst message by a beloved and respected pastor and friend, Pastor Hardwick from Christ Church in Nashville, Tennessee. I met nine-year-old Carlos in 1992, during my early years as a counselor.

Carlos had been removed from his home at four years old after being found alone caring for himself and his two-year-old brother. His childhood had been anything but childlike, raised by a crack-addicted mother who paid for her habit by working the streets.

Being left for hours, even days at a time, was not new for Carlos. Also, during those infrequent times Mom was home, she was not engaged with her children or emotionally present; she was high. When neighbors finally called the police because of the constant crying day in and day out, the officers found two emaciated young boys who hadn't seen their mother in two days.

In the newness of my career, Carlos' situation was hard for me to reconcile. I couldn't even begin to understand how any child could be living in such conditions, even though I knew at the same time he was one among many that did. Unfortunately, his story was not uncommon. I felt overwhelmed with the desire to take care of not only him, but every child like him.

I remember watching Carlos on the playground the last day we were together. He played games with the other children and bounced a ball against the wall for a while. Then he joined in a game of hopscotch, laughing and having a blast with the other kids.

He had a long way to go in the area of trust, and understandably so. Although we couldn't take back the physical and emotional trauma from his past, through the time he and I had spent together, the programs available to him, and the care of loving foster parents, we were working to give him a better future. We did our best to help him heal and give him hope and a sense of security.

I finally called him over to say goodbye. That day was our last day together. My voice broke as I hugged him, trying to hold back my emotions. I whispered, "It's going to be okay."

And at that moment, on that hot summer day in 1992, I made a choice to help boys and girls like him, however and whenever I could. The cycle must be broken. I didn't know how I was going to do it; I just knew it had to be done. Watching Carlos leave the playground, I prayed, asking for the Lord's help and committing my life to help other children like him.

After that experience, I did continue to work with children. It wasn't until five years later that Pastor Hardwick's empowering message entitled the BHAG – "Big Hairy Audacious Goal" – stirred a passion and an unquenchable fire in my heart, bringing my promise to God and a little boy named Carlos to life. At the time, I was Director of Counseling at Christ Church. But the Lord called me that day to begin what is now LifeCare, a new chapter in the Mauck family story.

Navigating Your Story

Let's talk about story.

"Your story matters." Although this is a current buzzword/phrase we constantly hear in churches and the counseling community, your story *does* matter. I believe that statement. I wouldn't have a job as a counselor if I didn't!

Every day, every week, every month, every year, sentences, paragraphs, and chapters are added to your story. The choices you make, the things you do, the places you go, the people who come into your life all add lines to your story. But that's just the surface. It's in the past events of a person's life where their story takes on a whole new level of meaning.

We can't talk about a life story without bringing up legacy. Legacy is the story passed down. It's the story you leave behind. It's the story that is left to you.

Again, all of us have a story, and it has been passed down *to* us, created *through* us, and passed down *by* us. You inherited a story. You are creating a story, and you are leaving a story. Legacy is all of these things. It's your life story of the past, present, and future coming together and moving forward in you.

Legacy and life imprint are intertwined, but not the same. Understanding imprint is vital to your story and the legacy you are creating. *Imprint* is both a noun and a verb. It's something that happens *to you* and something left *in you*. It's a mark on the soul and a part of your DNA.

Imprint can be both an impression in the mind and the effect of an action. When you *make an imprint* on someone through your choices, words, or actions (or lack thereof), you are actively participating in shaping someone's way of responding to life.

An imprint is something done *to another* and something left *on another*. The result is a mark, an impression, a *lasting effect*. It's a mark left intentionally or unintentionally whether or not either party realizes it.

Imprinting also happens through the events we live through or in, such as wars, natural disasters, and economic, cultural, or religious influences. This process has been happening for generations, shaping, and leaving a mark on your family and ancestors. And it will continue down for generations to come, long after you and I are gone.

Imprinting impacts an individual on a psychological and emotional level, which directly affects how you live your life. It impacts your story and the legacy you leave. The story imprinted in you, combined with your life story, is your life imprint.

Your Children's Inheritance

My original intent in researching my family history had been to simply make sure my family actually knew their history, that something existed on paper telling them from where and whom we came.

However, as I started researching, reading, and documenting my family history, the therapist in me spoke up and said, "This story is a mess!"

My internal counselor saw that in the lines of my ancestral history were all of the very same issues I've helped people through in my office for years. Patterns emerged on the pages of their stories, patterns I saw written in my own life story.

That counselor voice in my mind read the risks, the losses, and the addictions surrounding the names and events that had shaped my ancestors, their decisions, and ultimately my family. The scripture passage in Proverbs 13:22 (ESV) that says, "A good man leaves an inheritance to his children's children" suddenly came into a new light. The relationship between story, legacy, and imprint jumped off the pages, and I heard a voice say, "This is your children's inheritance."

During Christmas 2017, I had the opportunity to share some of my findings — ancestry, stories, and my thoughts — with my children and grandchildren. I told them of their seventh Great-Grandfather Hans Peter Mauck's bravery, of his parents' courageous choice, and of his fascinating journey to and life in America.

I shared heartbreaking stories of loss with a sense of gratitude for the sacrifices made by our flesh and blood ancestors who had a direct impact on our life today. To my surprise and joy, my family was wholly engaged — laughing, listening, and asking questions.

My hope is that I have rekindled a timeless tradition of storytelling in my own family that will continue for years to come. My prayer is that this inheritance of understanding our legacy blesses my family generation after generation.

Charted Steps

Your story is like mine, full of an inheritance of rich treasures and truths waiting to be discovered. Generational and eternal gifts are just waiting to be opened by you and then your children and your children's children. But for there to even be a gift, you have to start the journey.

I began this book with the history of Hans and his journey. His story and my story create beautiful bookends, if you will, to a chapter in my family's life imprinted story. As we fill in the middle, we'll discover the keys to unlocking your true story.

Many things imprint a person's life. We'll dive into those and leave you with a few things you can do to explore your story further.

IMPRINT — Your Family History

1. If you don't already have one, pick up a journal, fire up the laptop, and start discovering your family generation by generation. Start with your parents, your grandparents. Find a family tree template and start filling it in.
2. If possible, be intentional about finding time to talk to family members about what you are doing. You'll be amazed at the information they have tucked away just waiting to be discovered!
3. Cover this process in prayer. Lay your inheritance at the feet of Jesus, and ask Him to guide you, speak to you, and do His work in you through your family story.

CHAPTER 2

Uncharted Waters

> "Two roads diverged in a wood, and I,
> I took the one less traveled by,
> And that has made all the difference."
>
> — ROBERT FROST

MY HANDS ARE TIGHTLY cupped around my mug, absorbing the warmth on this chilly morning. The sun continues its ascent, further unveiling the beauty of the landscaping against the forest clearing behind my house.

The scenery is one of the many things I love about our new home and neighborhood. My neighborhood is nestled among tall forest trees, with many areas left in their natural state. I wonder how much it resembles the forested areas of the home Hans left in Germany.

I recently had the opportunity to visit the hometown of Hans in Toms Brook, Virginia. I imagined Hans stepping out and surveying his new home after arriving and settling in, much like I feel today. In my mind, I can see him also giving a deep sigh of satisfaction, of thankfulness admiring the beauty before him and the one who created it. Like me, he was probably humbled and in awe of the provision along the way as he reflected on all that had transpired and brought him to that place and peaceful moment while anticipating what the future held.

Hans Peter Mauck
(Continued from Chapter 1)

Upon any immigrant ship's arrival in Philadelphia, Pennsylvania, male passengers would be taken ashore by the captain, presented to the authorities, and required to sign an Oath of Allegiance stating their agreement to abide by the laws of the land before they or their families could officially enter the New World. So, when the *Samuel* arrived that August 1733, Captain Hugh Percy did his duty, and Hans Peter signed and received his papers of allegiance.

Within a year, Hans moved to Toms Brook, Virginia, where he turned to the family business of farming and raising livestock. Eventually, he opened one of the first German-owned lumber mills. On April 30, 1739, at the age of thirty-one, he married a young woman of German descent named Juliana Rheinhart. Together, Hans and Juliana took pride in working the land and caring for the home my grandfather built. Six children blessed that home between 1739 and 1760: John Peter, Catherine, Frederick, Henry, Andrew, and Susanna.

The story surrounding Hans acquiring this first piece of property on which the family was raised is both providential and humorous. As it has been passed down, a local magistrate with thousands of acres of land hired Hans to assist him on his farm. Colonial court systems were modeled after the British judiciary systems.

A magistrate was a local official in the court system, usually a British landlord and often referred to as the justice of the peace.

One evening after a few too many rounds at the saloon, the magistrate was so drunk, he couldn't mount his horse, and the horse became agitated. A crowd began gathering at the spectacle.

After several failed attempts, Hans intervened, settling the animal down and assisting his employer in mounting his horse. In front of those witnesses, the man gushed his appreciation to Hans and promised a prized parcel of land for his trouble and kind assistance.

Interestingly enough, Hans did acquire property a year later on June 23, 1742, a beautiful 168-acre parcel on Opequon Creek, deeded from Joist Hite who owned a modest amount of property and managed thousands of acres for a British landlord. Hans Peter would later bequeath this land to his second child, my fifth great-grandfather, Frederick Mauck.

A Declaration of Faith

On August 1, 1745, nearly twelve years after first setting foot on the soil of the American colonies, my sixth great-grandfather became the *first naturalized American German Lutheran Citizen* in the Shenandoah Valley of Fredericks County, Virginia, an act that would make history and set a precedent. You see, for Hans, coming to America was about more than personal freedom. Hans wanted religious freedom. Lutherans did not have freedom of religion in Germany, or in England. After signing the Oath of Allegiance upon arriving in America, Hans had a choice between two pathways to citizenship. The first and shorter path involved not only swearing allegiance to the Crown of England, but also swearing allegiance to the Church of England. This pathway too closely resembled what he had left Germany to escape. Under the tyranny in Germany, he had had firsthand experience seeing his family and friends refuse to accept state religion and suffer the consequences. Those who would not convert lost homes, land, and sometimes their lives. So instead of taking his oaths of allegiance, supremacy, and abjuration required by the British monarchy, Hans had done his homework and made a different choice. He understood that after seven to ten years of residing in Virginia, he would be grandfathered in as an American citizen *without taking the oath*. He also knew he would be able to freely choose his Lutheran faith.

One of Hans Peter's first acts as a naturalized citizen was to be baptized by a Lutheran minister. Why was this so important? The oath from here on out would be to God first, and secondly, to king and country.

These two symbolic acts, his grandfathered affirmation as a naturalized American citizen and baptism by a Lutheran minister, empowered Hans Peter Mauck.

Finally free from a life of bondage and tyranny, I can see the letters to those back in Germany. Not only would he let them know he had made it safely, but also that the voyage to the promised land of America had been worth every risk and every sacrifice made.

Frederick Mauck 1749–1830
(My Fifth Generational Grandfather)

Frederick Mauck was born to Hans Peter and Julianna Mauck in Tom Brooks, Virginia, in 1749. As a young boy, Frederick was enthralled by his father's stories.

As was the custom in those days, after dinner the family gathered around the fireplace for a time of storytelling, singing, or Bible reading. The most beloved stories usually came from the oldest family members — grandparents, great-grandparents, aunts, and uncles — of their growing-up days, the hardships faced, risks taken, and family generations removed. Folklore, humorous tales, and songs were the entertainment in the evenings. Legacy and heritage passed from generation to generation in this fashion, something mostly lost in today's culture.

Picture a spellbound little boy, enraptured by stories of his father's long and harrowing voyage to America on the *Samuel*, of his grandparents' great sacrifice and earnest prayers over his father. I can see him sitting at his daddy's feet, silently hanging on to every word as Hans acted out his exploits and adventures after landing in America, imagining he, too, is a passenger on the *Samuel*, a sidekick in his father's travels. Frederick determined that he will also be an adventurer, a risk-taker, and follow in his father's footsteps.

An 18th century house flipper of sorts, Frederick enjoyed improving the homestead wherever he was, and he found it profitable. He had an impeccable work ethic, no doubt learned from his father as he worked by his side growing the family lumberyard. Frederick appreciated and was grateful for everything he had. He knew from years of hearing his father's stories that life would have been different in Germany.

Frederick met and married the beautiful Margaret Schwartz of Tom Brooks in 1775. Margaret focused on their children, Peter and Catherine, while Frederick focused on business, and he excelled at it.

One thing Frederick did not excel at, however, was English. In fact, his thick German accent provided many funny misunderstandings and left his family in stitches from laughing so hard, such as the time Margaret had asked him to pick up some necessities in town, including a paper. (A little context for you...newspaper performed a dual function in those days. Not only did it keep you informed, but it eventually made its way to the outhouse for other purposes.)

Frederick headed to the general store, where the conversation might have gone something like this:

"Gerd morning, sir. I need pepper."

"Good morning, Mr. Mauck. We have that right here," answered the shopkeeper, pointing to the spice rack which held several different kinds. "Black pepper?"

"No, I need *pepper*."

"Um, well, then, white pepper?"

"No, no," Frederick said, waving his hands and slowly repeating, "Pepper."

"Oh, red pepper?"

"Nein!" By this time, Frederick was more than a little annoyed. "I'm looking for pepper for the toilet! I need newspepper!"

The storekeeper chuckled and pointed to the papers on the far end of the counter, amused by yet another humorous encounter with the funny German, Mr. Mauck.

Frederick the Traveler

When the Revolutionary War broke out, Frederick saw the writing on the wall. British soldiers commandeered homes, property, and even people. He remembered the stories his father Hans had told of citizens forced into servitude and allegiance to kings and warlords in Germany, and to the Church. Freedom of religion and freedom from this kind of tyranny had been Hans' parents' motivation for sending their son to America. To Frederick, it somehow seemed merciful that his father and mother had passed away a few years prior, not having to witness the very thing that caused Hans to flee Germany. After North Carolina patriotic forces defeated the loyalists in 1776, Frederick moved his family out of war-torn Virginia, to the safety of North Carolina. Once the Revolutionary War was over, he moved the family back to Virginia.

Comparatively speaking, Frederick moved more than the average American in his time. He moved his family across rugged terrain, from Virginia, to North Carolina, and back to Virginia, eventually landing in Ohio, in his senior years. Moving an entire household long distances isn't easy today, but it most definitely was not a practical decision in Frederick's day, especially repeatedly. Interstates didn't exist. Cars hadn't been invented yet. The family wagon was just that — a real wagon — not a minivan. Travel took significant time, and effort and was risky.

Sometime after the birth of their third child, Samuel, in 1785, Frederick and Margaret packed up the children and trekked to Philadelphia, to the port his father first landed in. He wanted to smell the sea, hear the sounds, see the sites, and touch the soil a young Hans first set foot on, to try in some tangible way to feel what his father must have experienced upon first arriving in America.

Frederick did have the heart of an adventurer and ultimately understood not only the risks in the stories his father Hans shared but also the value of those risks. His father's stories truly inspired him, as evidenced by the way he lived his life and what he named his children: Catherine, Peter, and Samuel.

His first two children, Catherine and Peter, followed tradition and were named after the immediate and extended family. But he broke tradition with his third child, my fourth great-grandfather, by naming him "Samuel" after the ship that brought Hans Peter to America.

In Hebrew, "Samuel" means, "God has heard us." The name "Samuel" encapsulated everything for Frederick, from the earnest prayers and enormous sacrifice of his grandparents, Wilhelm and Sophia, to his father Hans' long journey to America and deliberate "silent" naturalization and baptism. It meant freedom of religion, freedom of choice, and the payoff of faith and risk. The name *Samuel* embodied the legacy of his family.

More of My Story: A Leap of Faith!

Once the Lord spoke to me through that "Big Hairy Audacious Goal" sermon, I was all in. I created a mission statement. For weeks and months, through numerous sleepless nights, I prayed and labored over this new vision.

By that time, I was working as a counselor at Christ Church. After long days at the church, I came home and threw myself into writing out the programs on paper, along with the guidelines and services we would offer. I even included job titles with blanks next to them and mused, "Well, Lord, I wonder who You'll put there? Do I know them yet?"

Finally, the time had come to put feet to the pavement and move what would become LifeCare from a dream on paper to reality. I needed to start acting like a company even though we had no money, no employees, and no office.

I began our charters and bylaws with the Secretary of State in Tennessee. I did some research, and I found out we needed approximately $750.00 to turn in our 501(c)3 nonprofit application. Our current account balances were $100 in checking and about $650 left in savings. It was a sign!

Naturally, I immediately drained our accounts, appeasing that little voice in my head suggesting that I consult with my wife first by convincing myself I could ask forgiveness later. I took a leap of faith and turned in the application. It took a few days, however, for me to muster up the courage to tell my wife, Raye Ann, precisely what I had done.

Finally, I knew I couldn't wait any longer. I had to come clean before she discovered my actions on her own. I decided to take her to breakfast the next morning and lay it all on the table.

As I picked at and pushed my food around on my plate, a little too nauseous to eat, I explained what I had done.

Bracing myself, I waited, expecting her to respond, *"You did what?!"*

Now, pretty much any wife will tell you that would be an appropriate response. But my gracious and fantastic wife, while understandably surprised, instead said, "Well. Okay. But you do know that's all we have?"

To which I meekly responded, "Yes. I understand."

For me, the early years seemed more like a comedy of errors and mistakes than the start up of a God-given dream, and yet at every step, my faith was steadfast. As I walked out that promise to God and Carlos, He met me every step of the way, even when I didn't exactly get it right.

For Raye Ann, those first years were, shall we say, interesting. I'm sure more than once she looked around thinking, "Am I on *Candid Camera?*" Or felt she was in a never-ending episode of *I Love Lucy*. Only, I was Lucy. "Kenny, you got some 'splainin' to do!"

Everything but the Kitchen Sink...

At our first board of directors meeting in 1997, LifeCare's charter and bylaws were approved. I slept well that night. The baby, Life-Care Family, Inc., was born.

I tightly held to my chest those dreamed-filled pieces of paper. Even without names or faces, tonight the dream felt alive and real. For the first time, I could see our faith-based company was no longer a baby that was waiting to be born. It was a full-fledged toddler needing more space to move and grow.

I won't lie and say it was easy convincing my down-to-Earth, realist, financially savvy, and organized wife, Raye Ann, that we needed to empty our savings and checking accounts, convert our dining room into an office, our breakfast nook into a copy room, and get this venture going. Even more challenging were the weeks after receiving our first grant contract from the Metro Government of Nashville, a contract that opened the door to receive more referrals, which meant helping more people. It also meant needing even more office space.

Once I realized this, I began looking around the house, trying to figure out where to go. I landed in the garage. Yes, the garage would make the perfect office space.

As I explained what was happening and what I thought was needed to Raye Ann, I realized by the look on her face that this was not going to be an easy sell.

Incredulously, she exclaimed, "*You need what?*"

Now, you have to understand that my wife believes garages are for cars, and she likes to park hers in ours. To her, it is sacred ground.

I immediately realized I was on shaky ground. So, I carefully laid out my plan. Yes, we would have to come up with the money for materials, but we could have our fathers help with the labor, which would be free. We might be able to scale back a little on the dining room takeover, which I think is the point that made her agree to my plan, albeit a little reluctantly.

Once the garage was completed, however, I believe I fully won her over by completely giving her the dining room back. Also, while I would continue to donate my time as the president of our company, we could finally take her on as a paid employee at a modest hourly wage.

I'm quite sure it was not an impressive financial offer with her background as an executive assistant at General Motors, but it was a start and would be more than she received as a substitute teacher. Baby steps.

Time to Jump!

Between 2000 and 2001, it became apparent our small company was ready to leave the port of Christ Church and set sail alone. I met with leadership about the next season for both Barnabas, the counseling ministry I had helped build through the church, and LifeCare. We came up with a mutually agreed upon timeline, which included a gradual downsize in both space and financial support. The time to take a massive leap of faith had come.

Seasons such as these are bittersweet, and growth always has pains. Late in 2001, I had a meeting with all the volunteers and staff of Barnabas to get them up to speed. (Side note, leaving on a good note is essential. Always be sure you do.)

First, I wanted them to hear it from me. Secondly, I wanted to give them time to consider their own options. Many tearful and difficult conversations took place. Most understood, but that didn't necessarily make it any easier.

I was taking the greatest risk of my life. I had no idea that Hans Peter Mauck even existed then. What an encouragement his story would have been at that time in my life.

In some ways, it felt as if I was abandoning one child for another. Seeing God's hand in it all got me through the challenges.

I knew it was time to focus solely on LifeCare. Even though leaving had been a process, the risk weighed heavily on my choices and decisions during that time. Emotionally and financially, I would soon be free falling into the arms of God and letting Him catch me...the ultimate trust fall. That's a terrifying and exhilarating place to be.

But it was time to jump.

Navigating Your Story

I've been in some risky situations in my life. My cousin let me fly his plane once. Without telling me, he flipped the start switch, killing the engines and sending us into death dive toward Earth. I screamed. It was a joke and one I wasn't sure at the time I'd live through!

I've jumped off the high cliffs of Blue Hole in Jamaica, a considerable risk for someone with a fear of heights. I tried slalom skiing, emphasis on *tried*. It wasn't pretty. Admittedly, none of these hold a candle to the enormous risks surrounding Hans Peter Mauck's coming to America. However, when I took a chance and made the decision to come to Nashville, I was the same age as Hans when he embarked on his journey. Then when I took a leap of faith and started LifeCare, I was the same age as Hans Peter when he became one of the first naturalized citizens in the Shenandoah Valley.

Faith and risk are two core values, and I most definitely want to pass experience and understanding of both to my family. Imprints from my journey starting with Hans and Frederick stood out as a thread woven down through my family's story. In my experience, faith and risk go hand in hand.

Risk implies the possibility of loss or injury. Risk is often calculated as high or low. When we decide to take a risk, we are relying on our estimation of the situation, our knowledge. We determine whether or not we have the strength emotionally, physically, or financially to make it happen.

Faith takes risk to another level. Faith stretches us from the depths of our soul, a place where we are in communion with the One who is greater than all of our abilities and knowledge. Faith calls us to a deeper trust that involves letting go of what we know and what we can do *and relying on God to reveal Himself and take us beyond ourselves in His time.*

By Faith

If you haven't read Hebrews 11 before, take a few minutes and read it now. (I'll wait...)

What an amazing chapter on faith. Verse 1 reads, "Now faith is confidence in what we hope for and assurance about what we do not see" (NIV). Faith is the belief that something we hope will happen happens, even when we don't have all the answers, all the evidence, or all the information.

The chapter continues by laying out a spiritual lineage of faith, a lineage that is a part of my story, a lineage that is part of your story, an inheritance in which we all can take part.

By faith, Abel. By faith, Enoch. By faith, Noah. By faith, Abraham. By faith, Moses. By faith, by faith, by faith.

Every forefather of our faith listed was given a promise. Faith is the hope that the Lord's promises are true, that the vision He gives you is real and will come to pass, *even if you never get to see it.* You see, not one of them saw the promise come to pass in their lifetime.

My ancestors have forged a legacy of faith as well. By faith, Wilhelm and Sophia. By faith, Hans Peter Mauck. By faith, Kenny Mauck.

In those last days before launching into our new adventure, many asked me, "Why?" Why would I leave a position that had been such a benefit to the church and so secure for me?

In a way, they were right. The job I had at the church was a stable, no-risk position. I had been at Christ Church over seven years at this point and had a pretty good thing going. Why *would* I leave job security, financial security, and a comfortable environment for a job with little financial output and so many unknowns? Why would I walk away from the place where God had birthed my calling to our city and community? Why wouldn't I stay at a place where our counseling ministry touched the lives of hundreds upon hundreds of people through support groups, individual and group counseling, therapeutic classes, and a wonderful ministry of encouragement to single mothers?

The answer was this: The Lord called me out of it. I knew down in my heart I had to do it. I was called to *leave* just as I had been called to begin a ministry, regardless of the financial fears of myself or my wife, regardless of the concerns of friends over my decision to leave. In faith, I accepted all the unknowns and took a risk.

Fast forward about seventeen years to when I was on a trip with Raye Ann, and we were driving back from Virginia. Once we entered Tennessee, we drove through about seven different counties.

Tennessee is a beautiful state, and as I admired the rolling, tree-covered hills, something occurred to me. "Raye Ann," I said, "do you realize that in all the counties we have passed through since the state line, one of our staff has changed the life of a child or family for the better?"

It was true. Maybe it was that day, the day before, the previous week or month, but someone was providing medical assistance, counseling, case management, or trauma-related crisis support from LifeCare. Perhaps someone got a better place to live, help with meals, prescription assistance, a child was hugged to remind them they are remembered and special, or someone dealing with depression was helped to choose one more day; they considered living instead of committing suicide.

That little baby of a company we started at our dining room table in 1997, has grown into one of the larger faith-based licensed mental health care companies in the country. For over twenty years, LifeCare has provided counseling, in-home case management, site-based psychiatric care, primary care, adult and rehabilitative daycare, and 24-7 community living support services to over 100,000 Tennesseans, and we continue to grow each day.

With our recent merger, LifeCare is now part of a broader management organization that has over 1,500 employees operating in three states with plans to expand into five to ten others states over the next five years.

By faith, Kenny Mauck...

By faith, you.

In All Things

They say hindsight is 20/20. Looking back over my life, I find that to be true. At every hill, every valley, every fork in the road, I can see God in His sovereignty moving me in the right directions, His mercy correcting my course when need be. So many things that seemed mundane or outside of what I would have considered my "wheelhouse" were opportunities for training and growth. He was equipping me to be able to walk in my legacy story even before I knew what it was.

The leadership and management skills I gained during my time as Director of Counseling at Christ Church are invaluable to what I do at LifeCare: preparing for and overseeing staff meetings, coordinating family conferences, booking speakers, managing a larger ministry at a megachurch, and overseeing dozens of volunteers and paid staff.

And budgeting. I always knew how to spell the word; I'd just never done one before. Fortunately for me, Pastor Hardwick's sons, Mike and Steve, were in the world of business finance. Mike took the time to come in and train our entire staff on the ins and outs of budgeting. We were challenged as leaders to look at the needs and set aside our wants when the bottom line demanded it. Steve showed us how billing church members' insurances for their sessions could drastically help our bottom line.

Recently, I had Mike and Steve over, and we reminisced and laughed about old times. Both men have become good friends and successful businessmen. I shared with them that lessons learned about keeping a company financially solvent, having positive cash flow, and all the other financial tools they added to my arsenal had been invaluable to both the Barnabas ministry and me as I grew LifeCare, and they are continuing to pay dividends today.

One of the most valuable skills the Lord gave me the opportunity to hone is listening to those who came into my office needing help, listening to the stories of children similar to Carlos, listening to my staff and volunteers. By learning to listen, I also learned to ask the right questions and discern the needs of clients, parents of children, and staff, who helped shape the services and support that LifeCare provides.

What started with a promise and a mostly blank organizational chart that was spread all over my dining room table has grown exponentially beyond my imagination. When I remember who and where I was in 1994, and then look at where He has brought me to today, I am so thankful for the Lord's provision of training in preparation for what was to come.

I love Romans 8:28, which tells us, "And we know that in all things God works for the good of those who love him, who have been called according to his purpose" (NIV). All those in-between years, the promise of God working all things for good kept me going when I would begin to doubt. I would pull that verse out when I got weary or couldn't see where I was headed.

God works all things for good — the good and the bad, life experiences, job training, mistakes made, and lessons learned. I believe it is so important to "do all things as unto the Lord and not men" for this very reason. Your entire life is a training ground, preparing you to walk out your legacy for the ultimate purpose of bringing glory to the Father.

You have no idea what He has in store for you, what legacy He is working out for you. Don't you want to be ready when it's time?

Do Not Fear

As I look back on the stories of my ancestors, I have to wonder about the fears Hans Peter had to work through: fear of leaving the familiar — his home, his family, his country; fear of being lost at sea. Sailing was no easy feat and had no guarantee of arrival in those days. Would the ship make it? Would they have enough food, enough water? Did he have a fear of the unknowns of a new country? Where would he live? How would he live? Would he find work? Would he be able to make it on his own? What about his parents? Can you imagine sending your only child on a voyage on which he quite possibly could die, knowing you may never see him again?

When I stepped out from under the umbrella of Christ Church, I had a few fears of my own. Would I make it? Was I really hearing from God? What if I failed?

Scripture has so much to say about fear. or more specifically, about not being afraid. Joshua 1:9 commands us to be strong and courageous and not to be afraid or discouraged. God will be with us wherever we go.

Isaiah 41:10 also says, "Do not fear, for I am with you" and adds, "I will strengthen you and help you" (NIV). One of my favorites is Philippians 4:6-7, "Do not be anxious about anything, but in every situation, by prayer and petition, with thanksgiving, present your requests to God. And the peace of God, which transcends all understanding, will guard your hearts and your minds in Christ Jesus" (NIV). What could be more reassuring than the transcendent peace of God that passes all understanding?

One of the most tangible examples of risk, faith, and fear in Scripture comes from Matthew 14:25-31, the story of Peter walking on the water.

> [25] Shortly before dawn, Jesus went out to them, walking on the lake.
> [26] When the disciples saw him walking on the lake, they were terrified. "It's a ghost," they said and cried out in fear.
> [27] But Jesus immediately said to them: "Take courage! It is I. Don't be afraid."
> [28] "Lord, if it's You," Peter replied, "tell me to come to You on the water."
> [29] "Come," he said.
> Then Peter got down out of the boat, walked on the water and came toward Jesus. [30] But when he saw the wind, he was afraid and, beginning to sink, cried out, "Lord, save me!"
> [31] Immediately Jesus reached out his hand and caught him. "You of little faith," he said, "why did you doubt?" (NIV).

In the middle of a frightening, intense storm, Peter *believed* that it was Jesus walking on the water. When he was told to come, he took a step of faith and a huge risk. There were wind, waves, the small vessel being tossed about, water smacking the hull, probably spilling over the top. (Sound familiar?)

But Peter took a deep breath and stepped out into the whipping wind and choppy waters, and in faith, *walked on water*. Peter could not have experienced this life-changing moment without first having faith, and second, taking a risk by leaving the safety of the boat.

Charted Steps

Writing my own story has helped me realize the importance and even responsibility of passing my ancestors' stories down to the next generation. Unbeknownst to Hans and his parents, Wilhelm and Sophia, their choice set an example when it comes to risk and faith that still impacts our family today. I want my grandchildren, great-grandchildren, and future generations to understand that a choice made hundreds of years ago is relevant to their lives today.

As you are reading this book and discovering your family heritage, I hope you are beginning to understand that chapters, paragraphs, and sentences are providentially written to learn from and grow. Even the seemingly insignificant has relevance.

These stories are the imprints and legacy of your flesh and blood relatives, those with whom you share DNA. They are vital keys to a sacred treasure chest of meaning, purpose, and understanding for you and your family.

Friend, we've covered a two very important imprints in this chapter:

IMPRINT – Risk
IMPRINT – Faith

It's now time to break out that journal and family tree and put pen to paper. Ask the Lord to guide your thoughts and show you His hand and His purposes in your legacy story, your life imprint today.

   1. Who was the family ancestor who started your family's new beginning? For me, finding this person and following

the path through the generations of my family has been like opening up a treasure map to follow. Who are the brave folks you need to thank for bringing your family legacy to life?

2. What challenges or roadblocks did they face? What risks did they encounter? What was going on historically and culturally during that time?

3. Think of a time in your life when you took a big risk. How did it pay off? If you can't think of one, then how has the story of Hans and his parents encouraged you in the area of faith and risk?

4. Is there something now — a vision, a dream, a word — the Lord has given you that you need to act on but have been holding back?

5. You don't have to have all the answers, but if you wrote down an answer to the last question, what is a first step — your "leap of faith" — you can take to move you toward that vision?

CHAPTER 3

Facing the Headwinds

> "I am not afraid of storms for I am learning how to sail my ship."
>
> — LOUISA MAY ALCOTT

THE SUBDUED GRAY AND PINK HUES of dawn are softly fading, welcoming the golden tones and brilliant blue sky of the day. Manny, my Miniature Pinscher and constant companion, is curled up next to me, curiously watching me as I write.

Admiring the ever-changing color palette, I'm contemplating the impact of how one event can transform an entire family for generations. This is exactly what happened to the Mauck family through my fourth great-grandfather, Samuel Mauck. To tell the story well, we need to revisit Frederick and his wife Margaret briefly from a slightly different angle. There is so much more to uncover.

Frederick Mauck 1749–1830
(Revisited)

As we saw in the previous chapter, Frederick was like his father in that he liked to take risks and was driven to succeed. That adventurous spirit in Frederick looked much different in comparison to Hans.

Hans came to America and settled down in one place, the Shenandoah Valley. Frederick, on the other hand, preferred not to stay in one place. He loved to travel, to explore new frontiers, to set things in motion, and he moved his family several times.

The counselor side of me recognized Frederick as the classic middle child, a person seeking affirmation by outward action and accomplishments. Internally, Frederick was a restless heart trying to find his destiny through exploring. It was as if he was a ship seeking a port but not finding it every day of his life.

Unlike his siblings who seemed content to listen to and just be proud of their father's sacrifices and true tales, Frederick desired to seek out and create his own adventurous life story. This internal need manifested outwardly in the way he lived his life. He always searched for the more perfect place to live. He was driven, no matter the cost, to find an exciting identity like his father. Quite possibly, and tragically, Frederick's drive contributed to some of his most significant losses in life — the death of his wife and the death of one of his children.

Margaret died young and suddenly. Frederick's heart was crushed at the passing of his first and only love. He had not lost anyone since his parents' deaths nine years earlier. Now the love of his life was no longer. Nearly half of his years on this earth had been spent with Margaret by his side. She had been his partner in adventure and was the mother of his children, but now she was gone in what must have felt like an instant.

As a therapist, I would identify Frederick's life following the death of his wife as a significant break in his character. Margaret's death changed him. There would be no more trips, no more adventures, no more land purchases or homes built. Extreme grief and loss all but drowned his adventurous spirit for a decade.

Fresh Wind

Frederick's youngest son, Samuel, had met the young and beautiful Catherine "Caty" Hoppers. The couple had one son, Peter, before marrying in 1813, and two more afterward: Joseph, the middle child, and Paris, the youngest, who died shortly after birth.

In the years following his mother's death, Samuel and his siblings watched as their father quietly mourned. Frederick spent a lot of time with the family, enjoying his grandchildren. Sadly the spirited, go-for-the-gusto man who Peter, Catherine, and Samuel had known growing up seemed to have lost the wind in his sails. I'm sure they wondered if they'd ever see that side again.

About ten years after Margaret's death, Frederick had served in the military for a brief time during the War of 1812. After the war, he returned home to be near his children.

The great migration to the West had begun. The West was the new frontier. Every year adventurers seeking new beginnings, new challenges, and new lands set out with their families and worldly possessions in a steady stream of wagons from late spring to early fall. With every caravan's departure, adventure called to Frederick's spirit, slowing filling his sails.

At family gatherings, Samuel, Catherine, and Peter watched as little by litte, Frederick's spirit came back to life. When I think of those times, I envision Frederick sitting by the fire after dinner, telling tales of the Wild West, captivating the hearts and minds of his grandchildren just as his father's stories had captured his heart and imagination.

Catherine and her husband John's two boys, along with Samuel and Caty's sons, would sit at their grandfather's feet, hanging on to his every word. Whereas Hans' stories were adventurous retellings of what had been, Frederick wove wonderful tales of what could be.

After the children went to bed, I can see Frederick continuing the conversation with his adult children, dreaming of the life they could have, a fresh start, a new life, a second chance. Each conversation was more fervent and persuasive than the last as Samuel, Catherine and John, and Peter gave the whole idea more and more serious consideration.

It took a few years, but Frederick finally convinced Samuel and the others to make the dream a reality. He had found a new settlement in Scioto, Ohio, during the war, and he had acquired land for the entire family.

The hope of a new start brought new life to Frederick, a fresh, full wind in his sails. The family began planning for the three-month journey, set to begin in the spring of 1819.

Sparks Fly

After only three weeks of traveling, the rugged terrain of the Appalachian Mountains proved much more taxing on both the family and the horses than anyone had anticipated, including Frederick. The men realized that to make the remainder of the trip, the horses needed several days of rest. So, when they arrived in the town of Scott, Virginia, they made camp and settled in for an extended stay.

The first day in town, Samuel's older brother, Peter, met a girl, and it must have been love at first sight. For on the second day, he told his family he would not be continuing on with them. I have to wonder how that conversation went...perhaps heated, emotional. How could Peter do this, abandon them and break the family up? Leave them a man down right before a treacherous trip over rugged terrain? Begging them to understand, Peter promised he would rejoin them later in Ohio.

The woman he fell in love with and eventually married was Ellender Sparks. Now, I could not have dreamed up a better name myself. You just can't make this stuff up. Not only were sparks flying between her and Peter, her presence undoubtedly caused sparks to fly within the Mauck family.

Samuel Mauck 1785–1819
(My Fourth Generational Grandfather)

I can only imagine how Samuel must have felt. Peter was the oldest, the second-in-command in the family hierarchy, and he was abandoning ship. This left Samuel, the youngest, as first mate, not quite what the baby of the family had bargained for on this adventure.

However, Frederick was not a young man anymore, well into his seventies. As hard of a worker as Frederick was, he struggled to keep up with his young sons. John and Catherine had their own family and wagon to manage. Losing Peter meant two things. Samuel was now the eldest son of Frederick on the trip, and now instead of sharing the work father would not be able to do, Samuel would have to handle both his own family's needs and the extra work alone. Caty was a city girl, not accustomed to the rugged, unrefined conditions of traveling long distances in a wagon, and was focused on caring for their young sons. Frederick would be of little help driving, watering, and caring for the horses. Pressure began to build.

The trip to Ohio was taking much longer than Frederick and the family planned. To complicate things, sometimes the trails were marked; sometimes they weren't. Many of the passages were nearly impossible to navigate with a wagon, and the caravan would be forced to turn around, backtrack, and try another way.

The further out of Virginia and into Kentucky they traveled, the more complicated and difficult the travel became. They had to creep ever so slowly over each mountain and then carefully and cautiously down the other side, leaving them exhausted and completely spent.

Then Samuel had fallen ill along the way. With no access to a doctor or medicine on the trail, his illness progressed rapidly in a matter of days. He was no longer well enough to drive the wagon, leaving Frederick at the reigns for the final leg of the trip.

They finally reached Scioto County, Ohio, their promised land, on August 2, 1819, but at what cost? As soon as the caravan pulled into the small town of Wheelersburg, the local doctor was summoned. Samuel needed immediate medical attention.

Samuel must have realized the extent of his illness. As soon as the group settled him in, Samuel asked his brother-in-law John to find someone to assist him with a will.

The thoughts and emotions he must have had are hard for me to imagine. He loved his family. He must have been sad upon realizing he had uprooted them to move to a new land they knew nothing about, and now, he may be leaving them. As each breath became more shallow and difficult to take, every sentence harder to speak than the last, he dictated his last will and testament.

Whether or not Samuel and Caty discussed what should happen if he died, we will never know. The provisions of the will reflected that he knew it would be difficult for Caty to raise the boys alone. Being raised in the city and not familiar with farm life, she would struggle to work the land.

If that turned out to be true, that she could not care for the property and their boys on her own, Samuel asked that the family step in to help her. Looking through his last wishes, it is evident to me that Samuel fully expected his family to come alongside and assist Caty in raising young Peter and Joseph. He wanted them to become trustees of inherited property until the boys came of age should Caty remarry or something happen to her.

He also asked that Caty arrange for the boys to learn a trade, something from which they could earn a living and make a life, such as blacksmithing or carpentry. He wanted to make sure they landed a solid apprenticeship with a mentor that would train them well in a trade. Hans had been a lumberman and businessman, opening a lumber mill. Frederick knew carpentry and building, and Samuel was a builder as well. Samuel wanted the same promise of success for his sons, especially if he would not be there to mentor them.

Samuel wanted more for his boys than farming. Catherine's husband John was a farmer. In those days, a farmer was not considered a profession.

Samuel completely trusted his family to help Caty prosper and succeed and to keep the family intact. That's what family does, take care of each other...

On August 5, 1819, Samuel Mauck passed away at the age of thirty-four. Then everything changed for my family.

Samuel's death left Caty distraught. She was hundreds of miles from home in a rugged, fairly uncivilized, unfamiliar part of the country. She was probably not entirely keen on being there.

How would she make it here, a young widow with four-year-old Joseph and his older brother, Peter, and with no experience working a farm or land? In her grief, Caty showed no interest whatsoever in the will. It was completely out of the question for her to take on the working of the land. Caty was so intensely distraught, she was unable to care for her sons. In an act of kindness and compassion, Catherine, Samuel's sister, took Peter and Joseph in, hoping after Caty had time to grieve, she would be able to again care for them.

Unfortunately for all, this was not the case. Caty's circumstances were overwhelming for the city girl from Wilkes, North Carolina. In rugged country with a farm that needed to be cultivated from scratch, two young boys in tow, no means of income, and no husband, she struggled and found it nearly impossible to cope. In the end, Caty completely disregarded Samuel's dying wishes, severed all ties, cut off all communication, and moved on from the Mauck family. Giving up all parental rights, she left the boys with the family.

Within four months, she met and married a local man, John Halterman, and started a new life. She never looked back.

Joseph Mauck (1815–1891)
(My Third Generational Grandfather)

John and Catherine had not prepared themselves for the possibility of taking Peter and Joseph on a long-term basis. With four children of their own and a new farm to build from the ground up, two more mouths to feed, and two more children to provide for was almost more than John could fathom.

The last three months of travel had been physically and emotionally draining on them all. Relationships were already strained and in need of some repair, and they were now down two men.

The responsibilities left by Samuel's death and his brother-in-law Peter's absence in light of it, weighed heavily on John. How could Caty be so selfish as to leave John and Catherine to not only care for her sons but also an elderly Frederick and help him with his land? She knew full well that Frederick would not be able to take the boys in. I have to imagine John felt a little sting at Samuel's inference that farming would not be a good enough pathway for Peter and Joseph.

Stricken with the grief and guilt over Samuel's death, Frederick had become a hermit. Had his need for adventure ultimately caused Samuel's illness? Had he pushed the family too hard, too far, and brought this tragedy on them all?

He isolated himself from everyone, moving into the hills of his land. He seldom left his cabin and fell into a deep depression.

So, with the boys having nowhere else to go, their uncle and aunt, John and Catherine, begrudgingly and out of obligation took them in permanently.

I have found it hard enough for healthy adults to process grief, abandonment, and rejection. How do young children without any life skills or coping mechanisms process such things, especially four-year-old Joseph? He had been ultimately rejected by his mother, felt unwanted, unloved, and even resented by his aunt and uncle, and was dealing with grief he had no understanding of or ability to process from his father's death. Joseph developed a severe anger issue, manifesting in uncontrollable temper tantrums as a child. The tantrums grew into uncontrollable outbursts during his teen years.

The relationship between Uncle John and Joseph was rocky from the start. Joseph bore the full brunt of John's resentment and anger over the whole unfortunate situation. He gave preference, attention, and affection to his own children and even Peter, who seemed to naturally find his place in the family, while virtually ignoring Joseph's presence.

In John and Catherine's eyes, Joseph's tantrums made him a behavior problem that required harsh discipline. A good belt "whooping" was what he needed and quite frequently received. What they couldn't see, or perhaps chose not to see, was the abandoned, hurt little boy was seeking love and attention any way he could. He needed understanding and compassion.

Joseph quickly learned that negative behavior got the attention. As unhealthy as this thinking is, the negative attention to the young child was better than no attention at all.

As Joseph grew, so did the intensity and frequency of the arguments between him and John, and the chasm between them grew until finally, John had had enough. The anger spewing from this now teenage boy was more than he wanted to handle, more than he cared to handle, and probably more than he could handle. He hadn't even wanted him there in the first place.

It was time for Joseph to go. John sent the boy to a farmer in Elliott, Kentucky, to be a farmhand's assistant. Although Joseph had learned much from his uncle about the hard work of farming, this was not considered a trade. Samuel's request for the boys to learn a trade had not yet been honored, and now, at least for Joseph, never would be.

Joseph was again rejected and sent away to a life of servitude and hard work with little reward, while his older brother Peter remained with the family.

Silver Linings

Every cloud has a silver lining, so the saying goes. While Joseph's life would be better described as a full-force hurricane, there would be few positive events — silver linings — that impacted his life.

In the early 1840s, over a decade after his grandfather Frederick's death and two decades after his father Samuel's death, Joseph suddenly bought his own land and left the farmer to whom John and Catherine had sent him. How? Neither the farmer nor Joseph had any money, so how had Joseph been able to pay for land?

In his will, Joseph's father, Samuel, had portioned his parcel and inheritance to his sons. However, John, Catherine, and Frederick apparently never fulfilled this part of the will. I believe it was Peter, Samuel's older brother and Joseph's uncle, who finally did.

After Peter's marriage, he remained in Virginia with his new wife and never did rejoin the family in Ohio, while Frederick was still alive. Years after hearing of the deaths of his father and Samuel, Peter uncovered Samuel's will. In the process of discovering the story of all that had happened in his absence, he learned what had happened to Joseph.

Peter was now the owner of his father's and Samuel's land, and he knew that somehow, he had to make things right, not only to honor his father but Samuel as well. Peter sold what was rightfully Joseph's, found him, and blessed him with the money.

Imagine Joseph when Peter found him in his early twenties…angry, living a life of servitude, alone, poor, broken, feeling abandoned by his father and his grandfather. He probably knew he had been rejected by his mother, aunt, and uncle, separated from his only brother, and forgotten by his grandfather.

Enter Uncle Peter.

Peter told the story of a father who had loved his son, who had cared for his son, who had planned for his future. Peter ushered in hope.

Joseph now had an inheritance…freedom…the money to buy a home. He had *the love of a father*.

Like His Father before Him

Joseph eventually named his first child Samuel after his father, a sign that his adult heart had not only begun to reconcile the four-year-old's anger and hurt and forgive, but that he had chosen to embrace his journey. I interpret this to mean that Joseph now realized his dad had loved him, hadn't abandoned him, and had indeed planned for his future.

Joseph's first son had been born out of wedlock, but he would go on to marry the child's mother, Sara Holbrook, and the two would have many more children. Joseph wanted a large family. He wanted to be sure that should something happen to him, none of his children would be lonely or left alone as he was.

In all, Joseph had ten children with Sara: Samuel, William, Peter, Mary Frances, Sarah, Martha, Joseph, John, Amanda, and Jefferson Davis.

Even with the realization of his father Samuel's love for him and provision for his future, the imprint from the "father" he had lived with most of his life had been cemented in the fabric of his being. The anger was deep-seeded, and while Peter's gift of the inheritance and the repainted picture of Joseph's real father were healing steps, Joseph's heart was not fully restored.

Rage and discipline became ugly partners in his home, usually carried out with a heavy hand in the form of corporal punishment. Without warning, switches and belts were whipped out for correction, control, and submission. While Joseph desired to make a change, create a new life, and surround himself with loved ones, raging anger was the one piece of his old life he was not able to leave behind.

When Sarah moved passed her childbearing years, Joseph became restless. Children were security and safety for Joseph — the bigger the family, the more secure and safe he felt.

I believe he entered a midlife crisis, as many men in their forties and even fifties do, looking back at his life, mistakes made, and opportunities missed, and needing to continue building his empire, which was his family. During this time, he publicly took up with a younger woman by the name of Mary Ellen Rose and had two more children with her, Sampson and Laura Bell.

Missing the Mark

None of Joseph's sons were named after his grandfather Frederick nor were any of his girls named after his mother. Only two men of his German heritage were honored in the naming of his children: Samuel and Peter.

At first glance, it seems Joseph named Peter after his Uncle Peter, for Peter brought new life, good news, and hope to Joseph in a time when he had none. Joseph must have heard about the stories of his great-great-grandfather, Hans, either as a child from his father and grandfather or later in life from his Uncle Peter when he moved to Kentucky, after finding Joseph.

I find that revelation in his full name Peter Commodore Mauck. It seems Joseph thought of his great-grandfather as a commodore in a battle, a military commander, surviving rough and dangerous waters as he voyaged and battled across the sea.

The intentional absence of the other men in Joseph's life in his children's names was an emotional line in the sand. It was a familial dividing wall between those who had sowed good into the life he had and those who had sowed a lifetime of pain from rejection and abandonment.

Joseph left each of his children an inheritance in a small piece of his land. However, Joseph did not leave his children a legacy of purpose or intention. He had taught them as he had been taught — surviving in this world was a harsh business. The family business of farming was not a trade, which predestined generations of poverty. It was a far cry from the life his great-grandfather, Hans, envisioned for his family.

Hans hoped faith in God would be the most predominant element of his family's story. He wanted his family to have hope for a better tomorrow, supported by the lumber business he had hoped and expected to see his children carry on. Unfortunately, I can see from my vantage point that Frederick had missed the mark, focusing so much time and energy on the adventure and chasing tangibles — land and material possessions — that he had failed to pass on the legacy of faith to his children.

Making an almost in-your-face statement to those who left him behind, Joseph would eventually be buried with his body facing Ohio, the place his family had abandoned him. In his mind, he had fought the odds and survived despite the rejection of his own family. He made sure that through his crowning achievement, a large family, his legacy would continue in name and worldly inheritance.

More of My Story

In the fall of 2017, I lost one of my closest family members. My cousin, Landy Gardner, passed away from cancer. Landy was always jovial. He brightened every room and life into which he walked.

The morning I received his call with news of his illness, I could immediately tell something was up. The seriousness of his diagnoses was in his voice.

Landy told me about the malignant tumors on his liver and his upcoming rigorous treatment regimen. I sat in disbelief. It's true; you never think it will happen to you or someone you love until it does.

My cousin and I were like brothers. Not being there for him over the next year was incredibly hard. I encouraged him and cheered him on from a distance. I sent him scriptures and shared songs that I hoped would lift his spirits and bolster his faith.

At that time, I was in the middle of an intense doctoral program that required hours upon hours of study. I had worked incredibly hard to get where I was in the program. However, as the year progressed, somehow that pursuit of my doctorate seemed less and less pressing.

Finally, the need to be with family and support my cousin won out, and I could no longer concentrate on my studies at the level needed. Landy needed me, and I needed to be there for him. I contacted my professors and the Dean of Educational Development and left the doctoral program.

Over his remaining months, Landy and I laughed, cried, and texted daily. We talked about the important things in life. We talked about nothing. We talked about his cancer. We talked about anything *but* cancer.

I listened as he reminisced about what it had been like to be one of the premier interior designers in the country; about the times he did makeovers on our house; about his trips to Ukraine and to Israel; about how, when it came to dressing us for church, he knew better. With misty eyes, we recalled his and his wife Joy's choral arranging days, when their arrangements were used by churches around the world and about the thousands of people he and his choirs were able to minister to. He spoke about how proud he was of his two daughters, Dionne and Lauren, and how he couldn't wait to be at Lauren's upcoming wedding. It was a beautiful day!

Landy had a successful round of treatment. The tumors had shrunk, and the doctors were optimistic. He was entering a period of remission, but it was short-lived.

When the news came that the tumors were back with a vengeance, his prognosis was not good. The doctors proposed one more procedure, and Landy prepared for surgery. He was feeling weak and was limiting his time before the surgery to quality time with Joy. He had even asked his daughters to wait until after the procedure to visit.

I had an out-of-town business function and told him I would see him afterward. When I returned from my trip, I called to let Landy know I was heading to the hospital for a visit.

Instead of Landy, a dear friend answered his phone and gently told me that my cousin had just passed away. At first, I was distraught. How could I have let this happen? My trip had prevented me from saying goodbye to one of the closest relatives in my life.

Then his daughter, Dionne, shared his last hours and words with me. Earlier in the week, Landy had told her he had a lot of questions for God. As he entered the final hours of his life here on Earth, she believed her dad had that conversation with God, and God was answering. Throughout those hours, Landy would nod and say, "Okay. Okay." Over and over he repeated, "It's so beautiful; it's so beautiful!" God was showing him glimpses of heaven!

Landy passed away on October 28, 2017. I am blessed to have been able to be a part of his life, to watch how he lived his life passionately every day, how he traveled, experienced whatever good things life had to offer, and took risks to live life to its fullest. I will forever be thankful for the time I was able to spend in celebrating life with him. His zest for life, his passion, his expectation of godly excellence in everything he did and everyone in his life is a gift — a legacy imprint permanently stamped on my heart.

I have actually lost two influential men in my life in the last year. In addition to Landy, my beloved father-in-law, Ernie, passed away while in the process of writing this book. I'm still working through both, especially the latter.

I have seen my immediate family's experience of processing the grief surrounding Landy's and my father-in-law's deaths run in complete contrast to that of my ancestral family's handling of Samuel's death. We gathered. We remembered the good. We celebrated. We grieved, laughed, and cried together.

Initially needing time alone is natural in the grieving process. I can't fault Frederick for needing to retreat for a time. However, it's equally, if not more important to be with others who can encourage you, cry with you, grieve with you. Lean into the relationships you do have while you process the one you have lost.

Grief has intensified for me the importance of relationships, not just in times of sadness and crisis, but also daily. I love to speak with my parents every day. I consider it a gift to hear their voice and a privilege to be able to still tell them that I love them.

I hug my grandchildren a little tighter and fully engage when I am with them. I value each and every conversation with my adult children. Grief has helped me learn to live more in the moment, savor life, and treasure the people in it.

Navigating Your Story

Have you heard the saying, "All families have some level of dysfunction; some just hide it better than others?" My own father was completely unaware of our family history. It's an unfortunate truth that most families hide, or they don't talk about the ugly parts of their story. Unsavory events become secrets within a family, which in turn become fractures that don't heal, wounds that fester for years, decades, and even generations. A destructive legacy imprint is left with little understanding as to why these things are happening because it's never been discussed or worked through.

It's hard for me to admit that in my own family, my ancestors emotionally and physically abandoned a child. What makes it even harder is seeing that none of my family knew how to deal with their grief and loss in a healthy, loving way. They are not alone.

As a marriage and family counselor for over twenty years, I have heard and seen countless stories of child abandonment revolving around divorce or the death of a spouse, sibling, or friend. Sadly, it's far too familiar.

The Sins of the Father

Uncovering Joseph's unresolved hurt from loss and the anger it birthed has paved the way for a new understanding of my own grandfather and father, and ultimately, my entire line. My ancestral family's abandonment of a four-year-old boy had not only immediate costs to Joseph and his future family but so many generational costs as well. Neglect and abuse opened the door for anger and addiction to walk in and take up residence in our family line.

You may have heard a version of the phrase, "The sins of the father are passed down from generation to generation." There are actually many references to this truth in the Bible — the visitation of the father's sins on the children.

I think of Exodus 20:5-6 (NASB), which says, "...for I, the LORD your God, am a jealous God, visiting the iniquity of the fathers on the children, on the third and the fourth generations of those who hate Me, but showing lovingkindness to thousands, to those who love Me and keep My commandments." Also, Psalm 103:17-18 (NASB) which reads, "But the lovingkindness of the LORD is from everlasting to everlasting on those who fear Him, and His righteousness to children's children, to those who keep His covenant and remember His precepts to do them."

To me, these verses are widely misunderstood and misquoted. While these verses underscore the "iniquity" piece of generational imprints, they also highlight the righteousness piece. Was the "sin passed down" in my family? Yes and no.

Uncontrolled anger, fits of rage, philandering, and even addictions appeared for many generations in my family. So yes, sins were passed down. This is where I believe these scriptures are misunderstood or not given their full, true impact and meaning.

My years of training and practice as a counselor coupled with my own personal experiences have taught me that these are also consequences of choices made by those before me. As I have researched and sought out the Lord for understanding, He has shown me imprints left on my family that became generational curses. When my ancestors acted outside of God's guidelines and purposes, my entire family suffered many times over.

A legacy imprint was made that had devastating effects. Had Hans Peter's legacy imprint of faith and hope been passed on to his children, the events following Samuel's passing could have written a much different story. The choice of each generation to continue under the faulty imprint or break the curse, and with the Lord's guidance, create a new one is an inescapable factor.

What If...

So, what if different choices had been made? What if Frederick had embraced his daughter-in-law Caty and helped her see it was possible *to stay, that she didn't have to leave*. What if he had embraced his grandchildren and their mother and been the godly head of the family Hans Peter had been, leading the family through such a difficult time? When Caty left, what if he had stepped up and taken one or both of the boys when John and Catherine hesitated? At a minimum, what if he had been present from the beginning, active, and a help to John, Catherine, Peter, and little Joseph in finding and adjusting to the new normal and each other?

What if...

What if Joseph's mother, Caty, had chosen to stay and raised her children instead of run away from adversity? What if Caty had determined to stay with the family instead of marrying another man four months later? What if her choices had been for her boys instead of only herself?

What if…

How different would the story be if Catherine and John had just chosen to open their hearts to Joseph? What if Joseph had sincerely been welcomed and become a part of the family instead of being sent away? What if he had received affirmation and love instead of resentment and rejection?

What if…

Instead, Frederick left his family alone so he could deal with his own grief. Caty looked out for herself and left. John and Catherine did not open their hearts but instead held on to the hurt of being deserted by Catherine's brother Peter and resented being put in the position of having to take in her other brother Samuel's children. The unintended curse of abandonment and unresolved loss set in motion patterns of running, blaming, pride, anger, and feelings of abandonment within my family.

Look at the Psalm passage above: *"…to those who keep His covenant and remember His precepts."* To the chain breakers and those who make the decision to change the legacy imprint from one of running away to one of running into the arms of Jesus, you are the ones who change the spiritual legacy of a family.

Realizing the love and truth behind these scriptures and how they apply to real life has given me a greater understanding of my family and our issues. Piecing together the story of Samuel, Joseph, William "Wild Bill," and William "Tom" Mauck, both of whom you'll read about in the next few chapters, has shed light on some of the reasons people I loved had such anger, even generations after Joseph.

The importance of teaching our children how to confront fears and work through loss, not run or hide from, or pretend they don't exist, can't be emphasized enough. Even in the middle of the storm, God will guide and change our stories. We aren't meant to face these things alone.

First, we have Him. Our faith in Him, His grace, and His strength can create a love for each other that will become our family's strongest defense when facing a crisis or tragedy. In the end, only He can move us from sufferers of loss to healers of hearts, both our own and the hearts of those we love.

Compassion and Comfort

As our hearts are healed by the Great Physician, we are more and more able to give what I like to call "heaven-sized comfort" to others in their grief. Compassion and love are key in responding to loved ones in the grieving process or who are in the midst of severe trauma. In their grief, they should know they are not alone and have support.

I love the words of 2 Corinthians 1:3-4, "... the Father of compassion and the God of all comfort, who comforts us in all our troubles so that we can comfort those in any trouble with the comfort we ourselves receive from God" (NIV).

Friends, we don't carry this responsibility alone. This imprint of comforting others comes directly from our heavenly Father.

Psalms 34:18 tells us, "The LORD is near to the brokenhearted and saves those who are crushed in spirit" (NASB). As we begin reaching out to the God of all comfort, He guides and teaches us how to give heaven-sized love to others. He carries us as we carry others. He draws near as we draw near to the point that if we allow Him to transform us, heaven-sized comfort flows naturally from His heart through our heart to the heart of our loved one.

Comfort and love, even in the smallest measure, let alone a heaven-sized offering, was an enormous, gaping hole in the fabric of Joseph's life. The actions of abandonment and rejection by my extended family members were the very point at which my family, directly and indirectly, contributed to this rift. Too many things got in the way, including their own grief and resentment, and kept them from seeing first the true grief of Joseph, and secondly, the error of their ways.

Charted Steps

Admittedly, this is a heavy chapter. If you've experienced loss or trauma, if you or your family have dealt with abuse, infidelity, or even addiction, especially if there are unresolved pieces, you may have been affected more than you anticipated. Issues within your own family tree that you are still trying to make sense of may have been brought to mind.

If you haven't written a single thing down so far in our journey together, and this chapter has stirred something deep within you, now is a great time to start.

IMPRINT – Trauma and Loss
IMPRINT – Compassion and Comfort

Family connection is so important in times of loss. That said, sometimes so much dysfunction exists in a family that healthy connection is not possible. Many times, dysfunction is only made worse in the midst of loss and trauma. If you find yourself in that situation, leaning into your family of friends may be the healthy direction for you while you navigate reconciliation and relational health with family.

I encourage you to work through the questions below. Take time to talk to a trusted friend, your pastor, or a professional if that's what you need. Don't put off moving toward healing. You may need to change the trajectory of your legacy imprinted story.

I want to assure you that later in the book, we'll address a few other things in dealing with loss and its impact on your family. We'll talk more about the escape of addiction. We'll look at the importance of being a life giver in the healing process and being intentional in making amends with those we may have hurt and who have hurt us, whether the hurt itself was intentional or unintentional. It's a compelling part of our Mauck story and can be a powerful chapter in your story as well.

1. What losses has your family experienced that are still unresolved? Are yours or someone else's actions or inactions a part of the issue? What steps might need to be taken now?

2. What's the most significant loss you have ever encountered? Did you have the support of a friend, colleague, family member, or professional who helped you get through it? If not, consider calling a true caregiver or faith-based professional who can help you walk through it.

3. Have you or someone in your family been abandoned emotionally or physically? After reading Joseph's story, what patterns or reactions come to mind from your own life that trace back to being abandoned?

CHAPTER 4

Batten Down the Hatches

"When you come out of the storm, you won't be the same person who walked in. That's what this storm's all about."

— HARUKI MURAKAMI

YOU MAY HAVE NOTICED THAT for these first few chapters, stories are revisited. Why? Because generations do not stand alone; they build on each other.

This is something I've contemplated in depth during my writing time on the back porch — the intricate connections between generations. The overlapping themes and threads woven between generations are windows into not only my own soul but those of my current relatives and even my children. Learning about Joseph Mauck and his sons has only added to my understanding.

To that end, we must revisit Joseph's story for a moment to have a full picture of William "Wild Bill" Mauck, one of Joseph's sons and my great-great-grandfather.

Joseph Mauck (1815-1891)
(Revisited)

War, Whiskey, and Women

Joseph had many wounds from his childhood, the kind of wounds that do not heal quickly or easily. Even his desire to create a different life for himself and his family and the silver lining of Uncle Peter's return with the inheritance money could not keep the storms away. Joseph's outbursts of uncontrolled anger remained a constant in his family's life. The unresolved hurt remained an open wound that continued to fester into rage, and only became more entrenched and violent.

Until the war.

During the Civil War, Joseph was called to join Robert E. Lee's troops. Over the years he served, Sarah noticed a gradual change in his demeanor with each brief visit home.

The Civil War was a brutal, bloody war. Three million Americans fought; six hundred thousand lost their lives.

Joseph witnessed unimaginable bloodshed and uncontrolled rage fighting for his very life on the battlefield. No doubt he heard the screams and watched violent deaths, some most likely by the blade of his own bayonet. Perhaps his war experience began to put into perspective what really mattered and brought some level of healing to his wounded heart.

While I believe healing did happen for Joseph along the way, both through his Uncle Peter's actions and his war experience, there is a second factor to consider regarding Joseph's change in behavior. Truth be told, Joseph had traded one "vice" for another. One was developed during the war and would become a side business for him and his sons, Samuel, William, and Peter Commodore. It would more than supplement their income for a time. They would end up making some of the best moonshine whiskey in the Eastern Kentucky Mountains.

Whether it was the war experience or the introduction of moonshine, the anger was beginning to subside toward the smaller children. Unfortunately, the damage had been done with Joseph's older boys. Rage and alcohol were now close relatives of Joseph's sons. Tragically, his sons repeated the pattern and passed it down to their children.

To them, alcohol was an acceptable vice. Anger was the way to deal with everything. The introduction of an affair into Joseph's marriage had opened the door for infidelity to become the norm for his sons. These unhealthy seeds planted by Joseph grew roots that entrenched themselves into my family for many generations.

William "Wild Bill" Mauck 1846-1916
(My Second Great-Grandfather)

It's been said that if you walked down Main Street in Elliott, Kentucky, around the turn of the century, you'd inevitably run into someone related to the Mauck family. Now, I don't know if that was true. But one thing was true...the sons of Joseph Mauk were a rowdy, ruthless, brawling, women-chasing brood of young men, not a God-fearing, church-going family as their great-grandfather, Hans Peter Mauck's family before them had been.

As Joseph turned to alcohol as a means of coping with anger and rage, his older boys not only learned to run the business, but also to drink with the best of them. On any given day, any one of the

Mauck boys could drink any customer under the table, and they did and frequently.

However, it was Joseph's son, William "Wild Bill" Mauck, who took the business and the lifestyle that went with it to a whole new level. Being one of the oldest, Wild Bill was not one of the fortunate younger children who escaped the raging beatings of their father.

William had been there before the Civil War and bore the brunt of his father's rage. As many children of abusers do, he followed in his father's footsteps. Wild Bill's children endured verbal, physical, and emotional abuse far greater than he had been subjected to. More often than not, Wild Bill would be drunk, intensifying his rage and abusive actions, which was a major difference between him and his father.

Joseph was sober up until the Civil War and the moonshine when the beatings subsided. Wild Bill was three sheets to the wind drunk. Fear and intimidation ruled his home. The demeaning, shouting, verbal attacks toward his children were known to be worse than the physical beatings. Perhaps the only saving grace was at times, he was so drunk, his aim was mercifully not good.

William was known to all to be a heavy drinker, to enjoy a good chew of tobacco, and as a chaser of fast horses and fast women. A curse word didn't exist with which he was not well-acquainted. More than once in his drunkenness, he strolled the town square in his birthday suit. Yes, buck naked, not a stitch of clothing. Barroom scuffles, fist fights, foul language, and the occasional run-in with the police were not uncommon occurrences for Wild Bill or his brothers.

Despite his reputation with the women, one did eventually come along who seemed to be able to handle Wild Bill better than most. A young woman of Indian descent, America Harper, caught his attention, and the two fell in love and married.

America was a kind woman and stands out as one of the great women of the Mauck family. When Wild Bill went off on drunken binges, she held the family together. She protected the young children and was artful at redirecting Bill's anger and even occasionally diffusing it. America made the children a priority as best she could for the situation.

She also kept their farm going. Bill had never really taken to farming while growing up once the moonshine took over as the family business.

Still in Control

As successful as the illegal moonshine business was for Wild Bill and his brothers, one would think the family lived well. Pictures I have found on geneology websites of William's home, however, tell another story. The house was more of a shack with dirt floors and very little light.

Wild Bill never built a barn for his animals; they roamed free inside and outside of the house. He, America, all thirteen of their children, and the farm animals lived together right there in the dirt.

My heart breaks for the message that it sent to his wife and children. Even at the height of success in the moonshine business, no barn or pen was ever built for the animals. No floor or rooms were added. Nothing was done to show concern or care for his family's living conditions. Any money made was spent on Wild Bill's rowdy lifestyle, betting on the horses, or put back into making more moonshine. The business came first, and the still was always the priority. For years, this was life for Wild Bill and his family.

Unchanged

When the authorities finally began cracking down on illegal stills in the area, Wild Bill and his brothers eventually found themselves backed into a corner. They decided to shut the moonshine business down for fear of incarceration.

Now much older and not having any viable trade to fall back on, Wild Bill and his brothers were forced to return to their farming roots to survive. However, since Bill had never liked it as a child, he gave it minimal effort. His family's living conditions did not improve. The drinking and abuse continued. America and the children continued to carry the majority of the weight around the farm as best they could, eeking out a living from the land without much help from their father.

William "Wild Bill" Mauck died in 1916, leaving the farm to America and the children. According to the coroner report, cause of death was kidney failure, one of the possible side effects of liver disease caused by alcoholism. Sadly, Wild Bill drank himself to death, and his children had a front row seat to it all.

Such was the life and death of my great-great-grandfather.

More of My Story

Watching a loved one struggle with an addiction is not easy. Like millions of other families in America, I have battled alongside someone close to me, doing my best to support and cheer on their sobriety.

I've seen the daily battle to remain sober one day won but the next day lost. I've seen recovery and twelve-step programs embraced and followed, and I've seen them walked away from and rejected. Two steps forward, three steps back, on the wagon, off the wagon — I have watched the cycle more times than I can count from loved ones and patients.

I have learned through personal experience and my profession that family support is helpful, even essential, in the recovery process. In addition to someone trained and objective, an addict needs support from those who have walked through recovery before them to be truly successful. Surrounding themselves with those who understand the grip of addiction and those who have been able to overcome and find healing for the underlying causes is just as essential in breaking the chains of addiction.

Wounded People

Much like a wounded animal, an addict lashes out at the very people trying to help. My experience has mirrored this, as have the experiences of just about every family member and friend of an addict I have counseled. In guiding those close to the addict who are trying to support the recovery process, I always remind them of this truth: Wounded people wound others. I tell them not to expect a logical, or even in some cases, a rational, response.

In the early stages, you are not dealing with someone who is thinking rationally or is in a healthy mental or emotional state. The things they do outwardly will not make sense because they are impaired, not just when using, even when not using. Every good thing in their life is in danger of being damaged, sabotaged, or destroyed because of a wound somewhere that remains untreated.

In the book *Hurting People Hurt People*, Dr. Sandra Wilson discusses in-depth this behavior. Pain experienced in the past leaves a deficit, causing a person to lash out for no apparent reason at someone who has absolutely nothing to do with the source of their anger. For the families of Joseph and William "Wild Bill" Mauck, this was the unfortunate case. Events that took place, hurts and wounds inflicted by circumstances and family, cut deep into the emotional and psychological fabric and remained unaddressed and unhealed.

Joseph and William probably didn't fully understand why they lashed out so violently. Alcohol was an escape, but I'm not sure they could completely articulate from what exactly they were escaping.

Sadly, I have seen firsthand that it takes years for people from alcoholic homes to heal from the dysfunction of living with an elephant in the room, from hiding the dirty secret from the outside world of what goes on in the home, from the emotional and sometimes physical abuse that goes hand in hand with addiction and families. If professional help is not employed or if healing through the Great Physician is not sought out, both the addict and the family can potentially suffer long-term mental and emotional effects and even mental illness.

I believe William did have mental illness brought on by the wounds of an abusive childhood and an addiction to moonshine that only intensified over the years. In those days, help was not as readily available, and mental illness was not understood as it is today.

Over sixty percent of people with mental illness also suffer from some level of alcohol or drug addiction. My experiences in the mental health industry offer substantial evidence to support this statistic. When a prescribed psychotropic medication is not readily available, alcohol and drugs are the avenue of escape that many will seek. In addition, many choose to avoid the perceived shame of being diagnosed with emotional problems, rationalizing the overuse of alcohol as a less offensive and more accepted way to cope.

Navigating Your Story

An estimated twenty million Americans struggle with some form of addiction that requires professional help. Of the over 200 billion dollars spent annually on recovery efforts, eighty percent is spent on alcohol recovery programs. More people nationally and internationally struggle with alcoholism than any other substance addiction.

Addiction is an unfortunate reality for many, many families, including mine. I can almost guarantee that someone in your family, or someone close to you, is struggling with addiction. Whether it be alcohol or another substance, the problem is widespread and very real, and few of us live unimpacted by it.

The reality of addiction is often a shameful family secret, especially when it comes to an alcoholic. From the outside, everything looks fine. To your friends, your family may seem like the Norman Rockwell paintings: picture-perfect, put together, and well, normal.

On the inside for many families, it is the taboo subject that no one talks about. Family gatherings come around, and everyone avoids being direct. The floor is littered with eggshells that everyone is trying not to step on.

I've been there. I know the awkward discomfort.

So how does one navigate the storm of alcohol and drugs?

Healing the Wounds

First, by admitting the truth.

Here's the truth when it comes to addiction and those it touches: We are all the walking wounded. An even more important truth is that we all have hope for and need healing on some level.

Psalm 147:3 says, "He heals the brokenhearted and binds up their wounds" (NASB).

Twelve-step programs refer to a "higher power" in the process of finding healing. For me, there is no higher power than the Almighty God, the Great Physician. Thankfully, we find the pathway to wholeness in Him. No two pathways will look exactly the same because no two people are created exactly alike. No two life experiences are exactly alike. Some have addictions; some are the collateral damage of addictions; and some have been hurt in other ways.

...He heals the brokenhearted...

I find hope in the fact that no matter how our wounds came to be, no matter what our wounds are, when surrendered to our Father, He can and will heal them. He will heal your broken heart. He will make it whole again. He will make a way. He will lead you where you need to go through prayer, the guidance of the Holy Spirit, the Godly counsel and encouragement of others, and for those who need it, professional help.

...and binds up their wounds...

Binding a wound is a several-step process: Assessing the seriousness of the wound to determine your plan of treatment; cleaning the wound with fresh, clean water; applying pressure to stop the bleeding; applying ointment to prevent infection; and wrapping the wound in a clean, sterile bandage.

The same process applies to wounds of the heart, mind, and soul. The inspired words in this Psalm were not carelessly chosen, quite the opposite. I believe He is showing us that there is a process in healing: coming to Him so He can guide you, letting His love, grace, and peace wash over you, and assuring you of His presence and sovereignty in your process. Here is where you crawl into His loving arms in preparation for the rest of the process.

Applying pressure to stop the bleeding. Wait, what? Not exactly a pretty picture, but this is where the work happens.

When we submit our hurts to the Father, His goal is to make us more into His image, to "apply pressure" to those areas where work needs to be done, to apply positive pressure, life-giving pressure, cleansing pressure, purposeful pressure, transformative pressure.

Consider a diamond. Before it is that beautiful, precious stone every girl wants on her ring finger, it's an ugly, dirty, chalky piece of black coal. Only through a process of time, heat, and pressure does it become something beautiful. God wants you to be a diamond no matter what your wound is, no matter which side of addiction you may be on.

Whether addiction is even the issue or not, He desires to carry you through a process, to hold you when it gets hard and cheer you on in your victory. Does He choose to miraculously and suddenly heal some from the grip of addiction and deep wounds? Yes, He does! The how and why of who that happens to is completely in His hands.

I wish I could spout a formula we could all use to make it happen for everyone, one that would take away any work that needed to be done. Because we live in a fallen world, though, this is not the case. If His path for you is not immediate healing, know that you are no less significant or loved by Him. As I said, no two paths to healing are completely alike just like no two fingerprints are alike. He created each of us wonderfully and uniquely. Why would we expect our healing journeys to be any different?

Depending on the severity of the wound or the cause of it, more care may be required. To keep the wound from becoming infected, protection is needed. In some cases, this means the help of a professional to give you the tools you need to move forward in your healing process.

The people you "wrap around" yourself are also protection, people who will encourage you, who have walked your road before, who have become better despite their wounding instead of bitter because of it.

Charted Steps

This process applies to any kind of wounding. Is a professional always needed? No, not always. However, is pressure always required? Most likely, yes.

You may be asking yourself, "Why would anyone want to go through all that? Isn't it just easier, safer, to stay where I am, to live in what I know, even if it's not optimal?"

I would answer with a question: Is the legacy imprint you're leaving right now the one you really want to leave behind?

Let's get to work.

IMPRINT — Addictions and Deep Wounds

1. If you've been searching through your family history, is there any evidence of substance abuse? If yes, then with which family member? What effects can you determine through future generations leading up to your family?

2. Is there an addiction you or other loved ones might be experiencing currently? Have you (or your loved one) sought the support of outside help?

3. As you come before the Father in prayer, journal those prayers and the answers you are given. Hearing from the Lord could be as simple as an impression on your heart or a phone call from a friend that lines up with what you believe He is telling you. Remember this: chaos, negativity, isolation, and anything that is not in line with scripture is not of the Lord.

Note from the author: If this is your situation or someone you know, find help from a reputable place with exceptional outcomes. Success stories are an important indication of the effectiveness of any program.

CHAPTER 5

Wade in the Water

"The voyage of discovery is not in seeking new landscapes but in having new eyes."

— MARCEL PROUST

THE SUN IS HOVERING HIGH OVERHEAD. In the background, I hear the steading humming of multiple lawnmowers. The smell of fresh cut grass passes by on the warm breeze. Doesn't that aroma just take you back?

I don't mow my own grass anymore. Responsibilities of managing three businesses leave little time for any kind of yard work. Watching the lawn service guys go row by row, meticulously creating a pattern and covering every inch of my property reminds me of all the conversations I had with the Lord when I had time for that seemingly monotonous task. I kind of miss those talks. Epiphany moments I had while pushing the mower around my little yard in Flint, Michigan, eventually changed my family's course.

I am not the first Mauck to have that experience. My great-grandfather, Thomas Mauck, had his own epiphany moments. The providential hand of God was revealed in my family line through Tom, who allowed himself to be redirected, opening the door for my family to choose another path.

William "Tom" Mauck 1879–1966
(My Great-Grandfather)

William "Tom" Mauck was the last male child of William "Wild Bill" Mauck and America's thirteen children. While Wild Bill was abusive to all his children, being the youngest boy seems to have had its advantages for Tom. America had learned that if the younger children were left alone with Wild Bill, he would not handle the realities of a toddler tantrum or normal childhood behavior well. Tom was "her baby," and the two had a close, special bond. America had a soft spot for him. So, she kept Tom with her in the fields and on errands and around the house.

Consequently, Wild Bill had limited access to Tom growing up. Tom would be spared the brunt of his abusive ways because of it. Still, Tom witnessed more than his fair share of abuse as a child. The drunken rages of his father were a shameful secret of the family to which he was privy. Although not to the extent of his older siblings, he probably still endured a bit of physical and emotional abuse himself despite America's efforts to shield him.

In his late teens and early twenties, Tom was known to enjoy a good party, but nothing like his father and uncles before him. I have a feeling America was a positive influence in that area. Tom married young and had one child, Molly, before his first wife Luverina Parsons passed away. Luverina's death left him a young, widowed, single father, which caused Tom to grow up quickly.

A third-generation farmer, Tom did the only thing he knew how to do. He quickly left the party life behind and threw himself into working his land. Farming was what he knew. His daughter was his driving purpose, and he wanted to provide for her future in a way that had not been done for him.

Fortunately, his mother, America, was able to come and care for the baby during the day, leaving Tom able to work the long, hard hours needed. As his farm grew, so did his reputation as a man of integrity in the community, which attracted the attention of a young Dutch English woman named Mary Holbrook. Tom and Mary wed, and Mary took to Molly as one of her own, and she had plenty of her own. Tom and Mary had fourteen children, not including Molly.

After the death of his father Wild Bill, Tom made what I consider an extraordinary move. He sold his share of the 144 acres in Olive Hill, Kentucky, purchased a twenty-acre farm in Scioto County, and moved the family to Ohio.

I find this symbolic on so many levels.

Somehow, Tom must have had some knowledge of his grandfather Joseph's story and his Great-Uncle Peter's attempt to in some way reconcile the family. It's quite possible during his grandfather Joseph's sober moments, he had heard bits and pieces of the stories of his great-grandfather, Samuel, and great-great-grandfather, Frederick, as well as stories from Peter about Hans Joseph.

Realizing the hurt and pain his family had endured in Kentucky, he made a choice to go back to where it all began. To me, the move symbolized the anger and grief that had impacted his grandfather and father, and to a moderate extent him, was being laid to rest. Whether he realized it or not, Tom was reclaiming territory that had been lost both physically, emotionally, and spiritually for the Mauck family. The property he purchased was in the very same county his great-great-grandfather, Frederick, had chosen as his new settlement for the entire Mauck family, the same place his great-grandfather, Samuel, had died, and the same place his grandfather, Joseph, had started such a painful life journey.

All of this points to Tom being a peacemaker. Tom desired to bring peace to not just his little family but the entire Mauck family. He knew most of the story, had seen his own father's agony, and was ready to lay down the fight, let go of the bitterness, and start over. He hoped to make a new life in Ohio, and put the past behind the family. It was a history that for him started with his grandfather, Joseph, the baby brother who had died, the loss of Samuel, the mother who had abandoned him, and the grandfather who chose to grieve alone and leave Joseph to fend for himself emotionally.

Why did he wait until after his father's death? Perhaps out of respect. Maybe it was to stay close to his mother and potentially protect her from any harm. Or death brought a new perspective as it does for so many of us.

Whatever the reason, Tom and the Mauck family now had a clean slate, a fresh start, and it would change the direction of our family legacy.

Life on the Farm

Upon arriving in Ohio, Tom and Mary got right to work establishing a farm and their family. There were plenty of hands to help with the work, and everyone did. My grandfather, William "Lewis" Mauck, and his siblings worked from daylight to dusk every single day. Daily chores included but were by no means limited to feeding the horses, cows, and chickens; mucking the stalls; milking the cows before breakfast; and working the vast garden. Eventually, the garden became the responsibility of the children and after that, the grandchildren.

Anyone who lived on Tom's farm was required to work. Even sons and daughters who left, then came back as adults had to contribute. If they had a family, the family was also expected to do their part. No one got a free ride on Tom Mauck's farm. In fact, my own father vividly remembers inviting his friends over for dinner and on weekends, hearing Grandpa Tom's speech saying every time, "Everyone is welcome to eat around the Mauck table, and everyone is expected to work here as well." There were no lazy kids, grandkids, or even friends on Grandpa Tom's farm, and that probably added to its success.

When it came to correction of the children and even grandchildren, Grandpa Tom was a disciplinarian and could show his anger from time to time. His discipline was tempered with love and grace, though.

My father told me the story of one run-in with his grandpa's discipline. My father had not done what Grandpa Tom had requested in a timely manner, so Grandpa gave my dad a knife and told him to go cut a switch. My dad knew exactly what that meant; he was getting a whipping.

So, my dad went outside and returned with the littlest limb of a tree branch he thought he could get away with. Grandpa Tom gave him his licking, but I have to wonder if he wasn't a bit humored by my dad's choice of switches.

Ten minutes later, Grandpa came with five cents for my dad to go buy ice cream at the nearby country store. I believe Grandpa Tom grew up observing his father Wild Bill's behavior over the years and recognized it as something he did not want to repeat with his own family.

My dad remembers his Grandpa Tom as a likeable man and a natural when it came to marketing his farm's homegrown fruits, vegetables, wheat, and pork. As part of their duties around the farm, his kids and grandkids put together a wagonful of goods, and he showed them just where to hang the signs and how to sell their wares. If not enough items sold where they chose to set up, Grandpa Tom would hitch the wagon up to the old tractor and tow them down the road closer to town.

My father said Grandpa Tom was one of the hardest working men he knew. He knew how to motivate his young grandsons to be up and at 'em every day to work on the farm alongside him.

Revival!

In the early 1920's, a wonderful black evangelist traveled to the Portsmouth area to preach. The town was abuzz with excitement about the Reverend William J. Seymour from Los Angeles holding meetings.

Reverend Seymour was part of one of the greatest American revivals, the Azusa Street Revival. The Azusa Street Revival started on the West Coast and spread like wildfire across the country as Reverend Seymour went from town to town holding tent revivals and preaching to the masses. He spoke of surrendering one's life to Jesus, the power of the Holy Spirit, and having true joy.

Many experienced God's presence in their lives for the first time and were brought to true repentance. Thousands were filled with the Spirit of God as a result of his anointed sermons. (Reverend Seymour is also credited as one of the pioneers of the Charismatic movement.)

Reverend Seymour had come to Ohio, to preach in a Brush Arbor meeting. That night after some singing, the conviction of the Holy Spirit was heavy on almost everyone in the room, including the entire Mauck family who Tom had invited.

Reverend Seymour started to preach, and it wasn't long before people were streaming down the aisles to the front altar, not just for forgiveness, but to turn away from their sin and confess their need for true repentance and a right relationship with God.

Weeping, Tom and the entire Mauck family felt the holy presence of God, His acceptance, and His power. Some fell to their knees as they were filled with the Holy Spirit and spoke in tongues. Later, they described being in the presence of a love they had never felt before. From that night on, until his death, Grandpa Tom asked all his family to come to the living room to pray before going to bed. Every meal was a time of giving thanks to God. Prayer and thanksgiving filled the Mauck home.

William "Tom" Mauck had finally answered the prayers of Hans Peter Mauck and even Hans' parents, prayers for a legacy of faith, freedom, and prosperity. The Mauck family was now firmly back under the grace and mercy of his Lord and Savior, Jesus Christ.

More of My Story

The pressure of carrying on the family line is one with which I am familiar. I was my father's only son, so the weight of the responsibility fell square on my shoulders.

When my wife, Raye Ann, and I finally had our first child, Landon, I felt the relief immediately! At that time, I had not yet traced my lineage, so I was unaware that the last six generations of my family had at least one son to carry on the Mauck name. In this arena, there is safety in numbers. Had I known that, the pressure of being the only one left to carry on the name might have been even more significant.

Two years later, our second child, Megan Deanne Mauck, was born. I loved our little beautiful, growing family and the life we had in Flint, Michigan.

I finally had landed a great job working full-time as a counselor at the local community college. Life was good. But God's words to me telling me that I would raise my family in Nashville always lingered in the back of my mind, sometimes like an unwelcome guest, never quite allowing me to fully enjoy the good life I had in Flint.

Lawnmower Moments with God

Many times throughout those early years in Flint, I wondered if returning to Nashville would ever happen, or even if it should happen. At this point, LifeCare wasn't even on my radar. Any time I had just about settled in and gotten comfortable with my "no" answer, God would speak to me while mowing the lawn. Funny thing, cutting the grass. Lots of time to think...listen...and think some more. (Can I get a show of hands, men, on how many have epiphany moments while mowing the lawn?)

God used that weekly ritual as an opportunity talk with me, keeping the dream alive, assuring me that He had not forgotten me or my promise or His promises to me. We had many discussions on my front lawn, the Lord and I. Sometimes I would just stop the lawnmower and ask out loud, "Is this really You, God?" Now that I think about it, I wonder what the neighbors must have thought of this young man standing in his front yard talking to himself.

But the longer I stayed in Flint, the more entrenched and rooted I became. I realized it would take a miracle to get me from Flint, Michigan, back to Nashville, Tennessee. On the one hand, I was good with the idea of staying and hoped the Lord wouldn't move us. On the other hand, I waited to see what God would do.

After eight years of wrestling with God and my own doubts and excuses, I got to the point that I didn't even want to mow the lawn anymore. In those "lawnmower-moment" conversations with God, it was becoming more and more difficult to justify my inaction and my list of why nots.

Finally, I realized I had to do something to figure this out. I sought advice from two people in Nashville I had the greatest respect for and confidence in when it came to spiritual matters. I put in a call to Pastor Hardwick and his wife, Sister Montelle. Now, I had not spoken with the Hardwicks since I left Nashville. I thought if no one answered, that would be a sign.

After a few rings, much to my surprise, Sister Montelle answered the phone. I dove right in and shared my story, my promise, my dilemma regarding returning to Nashville, all the reasons I had come up with for staying where I was, and my concerns about leaving a good job and finding another in Nashville. I told her I just didn't understand why, after eight years of creating a life in Michigan, God was still after me about this.

Her answer was as kind as it was wise. She simply told me if God wanted me in Nashville, I shouldn't worry. He would make it happen. In regards to a job, there were plenty of opportunities, and He would lead me to the right one.

About a month after that conversation, I was cutting the grass again. The internal dialogue between God and I was so loud I couldn't even concentrate on mowing. Not even getting through the first couple of rows, I turned off the lawnmower and went inside.

Raye Ann looked at me quizzically, and all I could tell her was that I didn't think the voices in my head were going to stop until I at least tried to be obedient and send my resume somewhere.

I began exploring the job market in Nashville, focusing on elementary and secondary education. Honestly, I think that was my way of trying to sabotage the whole thing by not focusing on the colleges in the area. However, God's ways are not our own, are they? Sure enough, three new schools were being built in Williamson County, which is south Nashville, which meant opportunities for a job. The catch? Only sixty-five to seventy-five applicants were being hired, and over one thousand had applied. Well, there it was. How was I going to get that lucky?

Oh, I love my wife. She knows me well. When I shared this with her, rather than allowing me to accept defeat so readily and stay in my comfort zone, her response was, "Well, you won't know if you don't try, so why don't you at least send yours in, and then you'll know."

Inside, I'm pretty sure she was thinking, *Time to put up or shut up, Kenny. Enough already. You already know the answer.*

That was the wind in my sails I needed. I put in my resume along with the other thousand-plus applicants for a job with Williamson County Schools. I remember telling Raye Ann that it was going to take a miracle to get hired, that the chances were less than ten percent statistically, but I was going for it!

Confirmations

Even though I had my eyes on a counselor position, the next step in the process was passing the "National Teachers Exam." I traveled to Detroit to take the exam and waited for a call for an interview. Honestly, I wasn't holding my breath. With a thousand applicants to sort through, my resume would most likely be white noise. But to my surprise, I got my answer. The call did come, and I traveled to Nashville for an interview. That call was the first of several confirmations the Lord would give me.

At my initial interview, I found out the position I had wanted in counseling had already been filled. Mr. Ford, the principal who conducted the first interview, liked my background and experience and attempted to set up a second interview for another position as a fifth-grade teacher. If this second interviewer, Ms. Gamble, liked my resume as much as he did, he thought I might be a strong candidate for the job.

Before leaving the room to make the call, he said, "Kenny, I think you would do a good job for us. Do you want the job?"

I don't exactly remember what I said; I just remember being in shock and thinking to myself, "Did I just get offered a fifth-grade teaching position?"

About ten minutes later, Mr. Ford returned and said Ms. Gamble was very busy and would call me later. However, he wanted to give me the good news; I had the job! And I had my second confirmation.

I didn't know it at the time, but Ms. Anita Gamble was the principle of one of the brand-new schools. When I spoke with her on the phone the next day, she told me she trusted Mr. Ford's advice, and that, yes, she did indeed want me to be their new fifth-grade teacher at Trinity Elementary.

I couldn't believe my ears. Trinity? As in Father-Son-and-Holy-Spirit Trinity? The very essence of God was the name of my new school. At that point, I thought, *How much more confirmation do I need?*

As I sat in my car, tears streaming down my face, the years ticked off in my mind. 1983. 1984. 1985. 1986. 1987. 1988. 1989. Now in 1990, eight years after I heard God speak to me, I knew that this had not happened by chance. For eight years, I had pushed back, reasoned away, made excuses, gotten comfortable, but God had this door waiting for me. He knew all those years that I wasn't ready yet. Patiently, lovingly, and consistently He was calling, waiting for me to answer in obedience and wade into the water.

Within a week of returning home after my interview, the final confirmation came in a letter from the NTE. Nervously, I slowly unfolded my score sheet, and a smile spread across my face. I had passed!

I looked at Raye and said with great excitement, "Time to get our house on the market. We're moving to Nashville!"

The Big Move

With only a month to go before the move, I put in my notice at Mott College and got to work preparing for the big day. What I wasn't expecting was my five-year-old son Landon's reaction to the news. If it meant leaving his treehouse, he was not going. Now, this wasn't just any treehouse; it was a true one, the kind that wrapped around a tree high above the ground, the kind you see in movies. Landon and his friends played there just about every day.

One day, when Landon was a little sadder than usual about leaving it, I picked him up and sat him on my lap and said, "Son, if this treehouse means that much to you, we will build another one once we find a new home."

Trying to play it cool and hide his excitement, he looked at me sideways and said, "Okay. I'll go."

I won him over. He was now onboard with the move.

We listed the house through a realtor friend, but it didn't sell right away. Finally, I could not wait any longer; I had to leave to begin preparing myself and my classroom for the school year.

Raye Ann had to stay until the house sold. While we were living in two different states, I asked Raye Ann to make a quick trip to Nashville and find us a place to rent. I sent her off with a few guidelines. We needed to live near Christ Church, which was on Old Hickory Boulevard, and near the interstate.

To my delight, Raye Ann quickly found us a very nice condo and took care of the lease. When I asked her where it was, she could not remember what part of the city it was in, but said she had followed my instructions, and our place was near Old Hickory. I was at the school working in my classroom and didn't think much of it, but I was excited to go and see our new home.

If you're from Nashville, I imagine you already see what's coming, because you know about Old Hickory. Both the small town on the east side and Old Hickory Boulevard loop around pretty much the entire circumference of the city.

When I told a colleague that my wife had found us a place near Old Hickory, he looked at me, smiled, and asked, "Which Old Hickory?"

Suddenly my face felt hot. Oh, no. Had I been specific enough? What if Raye Ann had gotten us a place all the way on the other side of town, thirty miles away?

I ran to the nearest phone in a panic and called Raye Ann. She gave me the address, and I quickly looked it up. It was within a half mile of Christ Church and the interstate.

I breathed a huge sigh of relief and thankfulness for God's direction. For me, it was another confirmation that we were on the right track, and He was in the details.

Our house finally sold, and I went to Michigan the weekend before school started and moved my family to Nashville. Our friend Don Evans, his wife Barbara, along with Raye Ann's parents and some friends helped load the trucks and we were off. Raye Ann, the kids, and I drove in the car, and my father followed us in the moving van.

When we arrived at our place, more confirmation awaited us. Our new neighbors, one from Mississippi and one a Nashville native, were out front. Seeing us pull up fully loaded, they asked if we needed some help. For the next two hours, they stayed and helped us unload.

As exhausted as we were, we were so glad to finally be in Nashville with new friends who would become great friends in a very short time. But God wasn't finished yet; He had one last confirmation.

On my first day at Trinity Elementary, I met a man named Dan Finley, who for the last twenty-three years, I have counted among my best friends. Dan was the only other teacher specializing in children with special learning needs. And bonus — he attended Christ Church and sang in the choir that my cousin Landy directed.

I love how God just knows, affirms, and shows up in our lives. I didn't realize it then, but God knew that Dan would be a trusted advisor both personally and on the board of directors for not one but two my companies.

Perspective

Although I truly believed God had His hand in our move, and I was just glad to once again feel His peace in my life, we did have challenges. One of the biggest was finances. The move was expensive, and we were adjusting to one income instead of two. While on paper we appeared to have made a slightly better-than lateral movement with my job, Williamson County was in the top fifteen wealthiest counties in the nation. The cost of living went right along with that statistic. Our dollars did not stretch quite as far in Nashville as they did in Michigan.

Life has a way of piling things on whether we're ready for it or not. As if financial challenges were not enough, about a month into the first school year, my wife met me at the door after work with "that look." Guys, you know, *the look*. Then your wife asks you to sit down for a minute; she has something to tell you…

Raye Ann looked at me and said, "I'm pregnant."

The words hung heavy in the air for more than a few seconds. She smiled, waiting for me to respond. I sat there, unmoving, a deer caught in the headlights.

I knew I should be excited, but all I could say was, "Wow."

Not, "Wow!"

Just, "Wow."

Sensing my apprehension, Raye Ann attempted to smooth things over, saying she felt the same thing initially. No, we had not been anticipating having another baby, but she believed this baby was meant to be. Of course, down deep, I'm *sure* I was excited, but my thoughts were consumed with the practicality of a third child. I was already having a little difficulty feeding two children and paying the bills, so how was this going to work out?

Still in my stunned state the next day, I remember driving down the interstate through a heavy rainstorm. My thoughts were anywhere but on the road until a semi suddenly stopped dead in front of me. When my brain finally fully registered what my eyes were seeing, I snapped back to reality and found the semi's headlights and high bumper hovering right over the top of my little Geo Metro's hood.

Moments like these are perspective changers. How quickly I went from a stunned deer in the headlights to a father finding solutions. I thought about this precious little life, this baby growing inside of my beautiful wife, and realized I had not even come to God in the last twenty-four hours with my concerns.

I prayed right there, "God, You have given us a little precious new baby. I'm trusting You will provide the room and resources for this special life gift as well." He had brought us this far. Why was I doubting whether He had this covered as well?

Before our little Kelsey girl was born, our two other children were confident the baby was going to be a boy. At first, Landon was a bit disappointed; he wanted a brother to play with. Once we all took turns holding our second baby girl, however, she had us all wrapped around her little finger. None of us could ever imagine our family without our Kelsey girl in it. She was the period to our sentence, the last piece of the puzzle that completed us as a family.

God Is Good

As I am writing this, I can't help but be reminded how good our Lord is. After spending our first year in Nashville in the condo, our family moved to Smyrna, a small suburban town in Rutherford County. I had to drive over thirty-five minutes one way just to get to Trinity School each day, but I didn't mind.

With a third child, we had run out of room in the condo. Our new home was on a cul-de-sac that provided safety and room for our children to play games, shoot a basketball, learn to ride bikes, and of course, jump on the trampoline.

Just over year ago now, we moved back into Williamson County, to the very home this book was written in. We have come full circle. Trinity Elementary School, the school I was hired to teach at twenty-six years ago, is just down the road from where we live now. Much like Grandpa Tom's farm was just down the road from his great-great-grandfather's land.

Providence? I have no doubt.

Navigating Your Story

I have to wonder about Grandpa Tom's process in making the decision to move to Ohio. Exactly when did he first have the thought? How long did he wrestle with doubts, excuses, and reasons not to go? Did he even have doubts?

How much input and influence did his wife, Mary, have in the decision to relocate? What was the final deciding factor? What confirmations did he see along the way? What fears and apprehensions did his children have?

I wonder about these things because I look back on my own epiphany moments and see the process I went through. I see how long it took for me to actually step out in obedience and go, and I see the confirmations and providential hand of God along the way.

Be a Chain Breaker

While I don't know his exact process, Grandpa Tom's actions evidence an understanding of the damaging role the past had played in his family. At some point, somehow, Tom realized a chain needed to be broken. To not take action would be a detriment to his family. Staying in the same place, not just physically but emotionally and spiritually, was not an option.

When we don't realize the important role our past has in understanding who we are today, we potentially leave ourselves open to generational curses of fear and shame. Tom knew that if his family was to break free from the past, present action was required. He decided to be the chain breaker.

Deciding to take action is a first step. More importantly, we need God to assist us in healing from the past. We must be willing not only to confront those issues head on, but also to surrender ourselves to the Lord and take the risk as my great-grandfather did for his family.

John 8:36 says, "If the Son sets you free, you will be free indeed" (NIV). *We are promised freedom through Jesus.* When our hearts are surrendered to Him, one providential epiphany moment can and will lead us to the road less traveled, a place where God in His mercy leads us out from the shadows of the past. Taking us by the hand, He draws us out of the darkness of loss and victimhood into the light of His grace. In that light, God's ultimate desire for His children is revealed: to see His children, you and I, living in true freedom.

Charted Steps

Epiphany moments are life changers. Legacy changers. Trajectory corrections. It's never too late to change your family's direction. To identify those moments in your generational family's life and your own is to unveil the thread of God's providence, His guiding hand and purposes.

IMPRINT: Epiphany Moments
IMPRINT: God's Providence
IMPRINT: Surrender

As you think through these questions, thank God for the moments He shows you. Thank Him for revelations He gives, whether they reveal a positive direction or the need for change. Both are positive discoveries when surrendered to His purposes.

1. Has there been an epiphany moment that changed your family's direction? Were you or someone in your generational family the person who turned things around?

2. Was faith a definite factor in the decision to change?

3. Perhaps as you were reading this chapter, the need for a new chapter in your family's story was revealed to you. Are you ready to hear and respond to Him? Why or why not?

I encourage you to spend time in prayer, laying any hesitations, questions, and fears of change or unknowns at the feet of the ultimate Chain Breaker, so that you and your family can experience the freedom that is waiting for you!

CHAPTER 6

Course Corrections

> "Forgiveness is the fragrance that the violet sheds on the heel that has crushed it."
>
> — MARK TWAIN

THE EVENING SUN SLOWLY MELTS into the horizon, painting the sky above me from a palette of soft blues, beautiful pinks, and brilliant oranges. I wonder, when the sun sets on my life, will it be this brilliant? Will what I leave behind be beautiful, enriching, and a blessing to my family?

My thoughts shift to other men in my family and land on my grandfathers, my mother's father, and my father's father. So far, I have focused solely on the Mauck side of the family, but my Grandfather Nichols had such an impact on my life. My life story would not be complete without including him. His legacy will most definitely be reflected in mine as will my Grandfather Lewis'.

But the sunsets of each grandfather's life were so completely different.

A Tale of Two Grandfathers
William "Lewis" Mauck 1907-1985
(My Paternal Grandfather)

My grandfather, William Lewis Mauck, the fourth child of Tom and Mary, attended the tent revival led by the Reverend William Joseph Seymour of Azusa Street fame with Grandpa Tom and the family when he was fourteen years old. Lewis was among those who met the Lord that day and was saved.

Another family who also attended that night and gave their hearts to the Lord was the Frazier family. Lewis and young Victor Frazier became good friends over the next few years, and that's how Lewis got to know Elizabeth, Victor's little sister.

I often wonder what transpired over the next six years between Elizabeth and my grandfather. What started out as a buddy's kid sister eventually turned into a friendship, and then love. Elizabeth and Lewis were married in July 1927. They were seventeen and twenty, respectively.

After his conversion, Lewis dove into scripture, studying the Word intensely. He came to believe the Bible was the divinely inspired Word of God, in supernatural healing, and in the power of the Holy Spirit to change people's lives.

Two years after marrying Elizabeth, Lewis began traveling and preaching as a Pentecostal evangelist. In speaking with several ministers who knew of him while he was alive, I've learned much about his career as a traveling evangelist.

Lewis, along with his good friend and now the Reverend Victor Frazier, began ministering at various United Pentecostal Churches throughout West Virginia. Between the two of them, hundreds were baptized in lakes, ponds, and even the Ohio River. Lewis was instrumental in developing and growing churches in the Kanawha City area just outside of Charleston, West Virginia, and then traveled extensively throughout the tri-state area of West Virginia, Ohio, and parts of Kentucky.

In the early years, many recognized Lewis' anointing when he preached. Pastors and other evangelists saw him as a minister with an auspicious future. A highly charismatic individual who sincerely cared for people and had an extensive knowledge of the Bible, Lewis led many to accept Jesus Christ over the next eleven years, all this with only a seventh-grade education.

How I wish the story ended there...in the good years...in the years of saving souls and living a godly life under His anointing. Unfortunately, this was not the case.

My Grandfather Lewis was known to be a very good-looking man, full of charisma and charm. Coupled that with the fact that he grew up on a farm and only had a seventh-grade education, his preaching and evangelistic abilities were quite impressive and garnered him much attention. Eventually, gradually, pride began to creep in.

At the height of my grandfather's quick rise to local evangelistic stardom came a historical and sobering event for our country. On December 7, 1941, Japan bombed Pearl Harbor, and the United States entered the frenzy of World War II. As over sixteen million Americans, mostly young men, went off to Europe to fight Hitler, young American women were left home to hold down the fort.

The war presented our country with many issues, such as rationing of gasoline, women working men's jobs, and women also working several jobs on top of single parenting and keeping the household running.

Besides being a young, charismatic preacher, slightly full of himself, traveling without his wife, and preaching to girlfriends, fiancés, and mothers whose men were at war, my grandfather was also a pretty good handyman. Spending much time alone in homes without the head of the household present while fixing things around the house and comforting distraught women was a recipe for disaster. Lewis succumbed to temptation and had multiple affairs. It would eventually end his days as a minister.

The Truth Comes Out

When my grandmother finally confronted my grandfather, he confessed. Ma Maw Tess wanted to know every detail. Although my grandmother tried to forgive, forgetting was another level of trust she could never get to again.

Around 1945, after two years of coming in and out of the home, my grandparents had a fight over the past that was the tipping point. My grandfather packed all his things, and the next morning he left.

My dad remembers that last morning. His father kissed him and his sister, my Aunt Jo, goodbye. Dad was twelve years old. As his father was opening the door to leave, my dad was pleading, begging for him to stay. But my Grandfather Lewis walked out of the house, threw his things in the car, got in, and started down the long drive out to the main road.

My dad got on his bike and rode as fast and as hard as he could, pedaling feverishly, chasing his father's car down the long driveway, crying out, pleading, "Dad, please don't leave me! Dad, come back. Please don't leave me again!"

No matter how fast he pedaled, the car kept going. In fact, the car began to pick up speed, and my dad realized his bike was no match.

Finally, my grandfather disappeared out of sight. My dad was still yelling through sobs all the way home, "Dad, please don't leave me. Please don't leave me!"

My Grandfather Lewis continued to run not only in and out of the lives of his children but of his grandchildren as well. Without exception, I remember how he would ride up with a flashy new car and a new top hat and be off again within twenty-four hours to see another friend or acquaintance. His visits were always very short with a dramatic flair and gaps of years in between. Other than those sporadic, brief visits, my grandfather was MIA in his children's and grandchildren's lives.

Family Secrets

The truth is my grandfather did not divulge everything. Unbeknownst to anyone until years later, he fathered several children outside of all three of his marriages. Once I found out about them, I wondered if their experience was anything like my father's. I was sure that if Lewis did this to his first family, the same thing happened with the other children he fathered. The answer was *yes*.

Around 1974, my father took me up north to Michigan to visit two of his step-siblings, Laane and Lynn, for the first time. We all were supportive of one another, realizing the man who had so much going for him also had significant issues that he should have dealt with way before attempting to start a relationship with another woman.

Lewis never asked for forgiveness from my dad or my aunt or any of the family for that matter. His unwillingness to seek true forgiveness for the hurt he caused left insecurity in my father for years to come.

Room for Everyone at the Table

I would be remiss if I didn't share the tremendous respect that I have for my father's mother, my grandmother, who we affectionately called Ma Ma Tess. Ma Ma Tess was Grandpa Lewis' first wife and a light to the family in a very dark part of our family story. She, unlike my grandfather, was invested in her children's lives and that of her grandchildren and great-grandchildren. Both my father and my Aunt Jolene have said on numerous occasions that had it not been for their mother, they would not have made it through those tumultuous years.

My grandmother wasn't just known as Ma Ma Tess by her family. Everyone called her Ma Ma Tess. My grandparents lived through the Great Depression, but there was always enough food for everyone who found themselves around Ma Ma Tess's table. She would stand for hours if needed in the food lines to make sure family and friends had enough. Quality time was a priority, and she was sure to spend it with everyone who came to visit.

Ma Ma Tess made sure everyone in the family attended church. She made sure the family knew proper etiquette, including how to properly set up a dining room and proper placement of the silverware on a place setting. She danced with us, sang songs with us, played games with us, rode her bike right next to us, always had a spoon handy to give us a taste of her latest concoction, which was always amazing.

She lived her whole life to love God, her family, and children. Ma Ma Tess was a mom to all.

Ma Ma Tess never stopped loving Lewis, our grandfather. Three times after their divorce, she attempted to get back together and reconcile the relationship. The last time, she took care of him during his final months of life. What a gracious, loving woman she was. I think I speak on behalf of all of my siblings and cousins when I say Ma Ma Tess was, and always will remain one of the most loving, special relatives we have ever known.

Marcus "Pa Paw" Nichols 1900–1999
(My Maternal Grandfather)

My mother's father, Pa Paw Nichols from Louisiana, couldn't have been more different than my Grandpa Lewis. Marcus "Mark" Nichols stood at only five foot seven inches tall, but to me, he stood seven feet tall. Pa Paw was one of the most significant influencers of my life as a child.

He represented to me all that a grandpa should be, what a grandfather looks like, smells like, and acts like. His gentle nature, demeanor, and love for the underdog were unmatched. He was laid back, funny as all get out, and loved his grandkids. He was the grandpa every kid wanted to have and the grandpa I strive to be.

My Ma Maw, Merta Mae Nichols, was one of the toughest women I had ever met. Her outlook on life was relatively black and white. Not many gray areas existed in the world for Ma Maw, and that made for some entertaining conversations over the years. Both my Ma Maw and Pa Paw were two of the greatest examples of faith I ever met.

Every minute of the almost twenty-hour drive to their home in De-Ridder, Louisiana, was forgotten as soon as we entered the house. Pa Paw and Ma Maw always had dinner planned and spent hours preparing for our arrival at the table. Tired and starving, we raced to the front door, clamoring to be the first to savor the tantalizing aromas of bona fide southern cooking. The beautiful buffet of pot roast, ham, fresh sweet potatoes, green beans, black-eyed peas, greens, mashed potatoes and gravy, corn on the cob, and scrumptious banana creme and pecan pies filled every inch of the table. The feast continued all week with peach cobbler, banana pudding (a Southern staple), and the best homemade jam and homemade ice cream you ever put in your mouth, too. Oh, yeah! The long day that started in the wee hours and all those hours of driving was always worth it once we hit Roberts Street.

As good as all that food was, after dinner was my favorite time. I would shadow my Pa Paw, following him out to his impressive garden that grew bigger each time we visited. His homegrown tomatoes were the best in the world.

To me, Mark Nichols was and remains a man among men. We would walk through the garden, and he would tell me all the different vegetables he was growing each year.

The weather was about one hundred degrees in the shade, so Ma Maw always had fresh-squeezed lemonade waiting for us. Pa Paw would sit me down and fill me in on everything he had done to his old '57 Plymouth since our last visit. Paid off some twenty years earlier, the car still looked brand-spanking new with the same hard plastic covers to keep the seats clean, and it ran like a champ. An oil change was never missed and always happened at 3,000 miles on the dot. I'm still amazed at just how neat and clean that car was.

Looking back over my time with Pa Paw, I realize his main influence on my life came from watching how he lived his life. You see, he was the neighborhood social worker and handyman for a widow or single mom. He simply fixed broken windows and doors that jammed at the bottom, or he would cut down a stubborn tree after a windy storm. There was no fanfare, and he was always respectful and honorable, never out of line with anyone. He never once told me why he had to go down the street for a while, but my mom and grandmother would.

I will never forget watching my grandfather lovingly care for my Ma Maw as best as he could when she was diagnosed with dementia in her late sixties. She eventually passed away in 1982. I was twenty-three. I remember thinking after going to her funeral that Grandfather would finally have some time to rest and what relief he must be feeling. But that night, he demanded my parents remain in his full-size bed. Then right before he crawled into the other twin bed in the guest room where I was staying, I overheard his prayer. It will forever be etched in my mind.

His voice broke and was thick with emotion as he prayed:

"Dear Lord, thank You for all the wonderful years You gave me and Merta Mae together, for these have been some of the best years of my life."

Laying silently in the dark in the other twin bed, I couldn't stop the tears. We had buried his sweetheart of sixty-two years, the last thirteen of which had been some of the hardest of his life. He had cared for Ma Maw and watched her illness progress to the point of not recognizing him or any of her family anymore.

My grandfather's prayer spoke volumes to me. He loved Ma Maw in sickness and in health and continued to love her until his death ten years later, a few weeks before his ninety-ninth birthday. He always remained committed in love and faithful to his one and only wife.

More of My Story

My two grandfathers have both left lasting imprints on my life, albeit very different ones. With God's help, I hope both are passed down through me as positive imprints on my own family.

Looking back, I hurt for my father. Many times, he has told me how painful it was to never see his father reconcile with the family. Because of the emotional hurt he experienced growing up, going to bed at night with an absent father, Dad vowed never to do the same to his children. At least fifty times my dad told us mom could kick him out of the bedroom but never out of the home. He never wanted his children to feel the pain he had coming from a broken home.

Immediate and extended family, myself included, have continued to struggle with forgiving my grandfather for the damage he caused. He never could come to terms with his own past and never asked those whom he harmed for forgiveness. Just as importantly, I do not believe he ever did truly forgive himself. Instead of facing his issues, he ran. My grandfather ran from place to place, from woman to woman, from distraction to distraction, never really stopping to ask himself why. His running left a trail of heartache and brokenness for all of his children.

At my Pa Paw Nichols' funeral, I was asked to share a few words. In front of a packed church auditorium, I shared stories I had heard of him seeing the first car ever to come down the streets of DeRidder, of racing through town on his horse, letting everyone know we were at war. I told of his service in World War II, deep in the hulls of our navy ships as a welder, nailing down and making sure the massive ship engines were secure.

At the end of my eulogy, I looked out at all those in the audience who had taken time off from work, even traveled great distances to be there to honor my Pa Paw, the majority of whom I did not know. I thanked them for coming.

As I stepped down from the stage, I kissed my grandfather on his forehead as he had done for me so many times when I was a young boy about to go to sleep.

On my ride back home to Tennessee, I thought about my two grandfathers. I couldn't help but compare and contrast their passings. One of my grandfathers preached and baptized hundreds, even thousands, very publicly all over Ohio. Yet few, if any, came to see him when he was ill in South Point, Ohio, or when we buried him in the Friendship, Ohio Cemetery. In contrast, my Pa Paw

Nichols cared for those no one in the church even knew about, and the families of those he touched never forgot. Even though most of those he actually helped were gone years before him, their families came to honor him.

Navigating Your Story

On a recent trip to New York, I experienced Uber for the first time, and I had some interesting conversations with three of my eight drivers. Once these drivers found out I was a counselor, they began pouring out their hearts, sharing their stories.

One was struggling with his wife's over-commitment and lack of investment in the relationship that led to divorce. The second man was missing his children now that he and his wife were separated, and the third spoke of past unresolved issues with his family.

I listened intently to each one, reading between the lines of what they were saying. Each story was completely different, yet all had a common thread. Each needed resolution, to make amends with a family member and the past.

Forgive...Me

A few months ago while laboring over my Grandfather Lewis Mauck's past indiscretions, I realized I needed to make some amends myself. It was time for me to finally come to grips with the family secret. Years of guilt and shame hovered over my father, my aunt, and Lewis's grandchildren — Landy, Ronda, Jonda, Candy, Tammy, and myself. My turn had come to face down my family's generational curses and the iniquities passed down over the generations from Joseph, William "Wild Bill," and now my Grandfather Lewis.

As I prepared myself, I thought, *I'm going to forgive each of these men for the great pain they have inflicted not only on their own spouses and children but also for what they did to my father and me as well.* In my mind, I was going to right all the wrongs through my prayer and devotional time and finally rid myself of all this "stuff."

When I was about to pray, God's presence overwhelmed me, and I felt a sincere sense of conviction. The words that came out of my mouth and the stirring in my heart were completely different from what I had thought I would be praying. How great is our God! He gently yet powerfully showed me that I had other steps I personally needed to take for true amends to be made, steps that looked nothing like what I had envisioned.

He spoke to my heart and said, "Kenny, you have work to do before pointing fingers at your grandfathers."

As a result, my prayer actually began like this:

"Father in Heaven,

"Forgive me. I must first make amends with You before I can confront another who has wronged me. Forgive me for my greed, lust, pride, and false sense of control. I have hurt my relationship with You due to my actions, and I ask Your forgiveness.

"Lord, I also know my lack of true repentance has caused my wife, children, grandchildren, and friends pain as a result of my not being totally broken about my own sin. Because I have not come to You sooner, my actions may have caused those I love frustration, anger, and hurt. I ask You to give me the opportunity to make it right. If there is anyone I have hurt as a result of my own unresolved loss and hurt, please reveal them to me so that I may seek forgiveness."

As I began to pray, tears streamed down my face. I realized God would not minimize my own offenses and sins just because I had not fathered a child or had sex outside of my marriage. God was having none of my effort to make things right with my grandfather until my own vessel was cleaned out first.

The Lord reminded me of a phrase I had learned while training with Steven Covey. "Seek first to understand, then to be understood." This phrase accentuated the steps I needed to walk, first in seeking true forgiveness. It was vital that I first seek the grace of God for myself before ever thinking about plucking the blinders off my generational family.

Isn't that just like our God – to get right to the heart of the matter and be more concerned about what we need from Him over what we need from others?

The Empty Chair

My greatest hurt regarding my Grandpa Lewis still needed to be confronted, but not from a place of anger. After some thought, I wrote a letter and planned to read it to my deceased grandfather. Letter writing is something I have had many do to make amends with a deceased relative.

To facilitate the process, I decided to use another exercise I have taken many through when confronting an unresolved loss, the "Empty Chair." The empty chair represents the person removed from your life in some way, but their actions continue to have a hold on you. This might include one's raw feelings as a result of a horrible divorce, a death, or a separation.

I placed an old picture of my grandfather in the empty chair and sat there staring at it for a few moments. Then I took a deep breath and began:

"Grandpa Mauck, I realize you are not physically here, but this is the closet way I can create a real conversation between us now. I remember seeing you once at my pee-wee football practice in Mobile, Alabama, wearing your fedora hat. Your visits with my dad, mom, and us grandchildren, as I recall, were always very short. It seemed you were

constantly on the run, coming in around time for lunch and gone by evening or before we got up the next morning.

"Because you needed to work the fields on the farm in Portsmouth, you only completed school through the seventh grade. Being the oldest male of twelve children probably meant more was required of you. At the age of twenty, you married my grandma, Ma Ma Tess, and felt called to ministry as a result of Reverend Seymour's tent revival. In the early years, your ministry actually flourished as evidenced by the number of people saved and baptized. You did some wonderful things, but somewhere around the age of thirty-five, your charisma and good looks gave way to pride, ego, and a lust for women.

"I am not trying to judge you, but my dad tearfully revealed to me a family secret, something that happened when he was twelve years old, a secret you have withheld from the family and me. Not only did I find out how you actually left Ma Ma Tess, my dad, and his sister, Aunt Jolene, about twelve years ago, I found out from my dad that you fathered two other precious children, Laane and Lynn.

"Just this last year around dad's eighty-fifth birthday, news of two additional children you fathered came to light. My dad, while very surprised, took the news well and wanted to make contact with his newly discovered siblings. My sister and I also wanted to reach out to these new relatives. Fortunately, my dad, my sister Candy, and I were able to connect with them. None of this really surprised me, but I feel let down that you kept this secret from my dad and the rest of the family. I wish you could have reconciled and trusted your family instead of keeping secrets. Your daughter, Cynthia, shared that she remembers you doting on her but was never told you were her father until many years later as an adult. Jerry was a son you never met.

"My desire is not at all to shame you, but I watched my own father suffer emotionally, seeking affirmation and attention from people as a result of your absence throughout most of his life. I know from being a counselor that an absent father combined with a broken home is one the hardest things for a child to overcome. Without God's grace, all of your children *could have grown up with hardened feelings of unresolved loss. Each family member has had to come to terms in their own way, finding their own path to forgive you as I am doing today.*

"I don't want there to be any more untold secrets that will impact my father, children, or grandchildren. So, I am letting you know, Grandpa, that I am releasing you and myself from guilt or shame.

"I hope that before you left this earth, you asked God to forgive you for all the hurts you caused, both to yourself and to others. When all is said and done, I pray you found peace for your soul, as we have had to find as well.

Kenny

God has been so faithful in this process of acknowledging my own need for forgiveness and in finding it in my heart to forgive my grandfather. With every honest step I take toward true reconciliation and wholeness, He meets me with peace, healing, and such grace. His faithfulness to me — to my walk as a believer, to making me more in His image through the process — is ongoing and a treasured part of my journey.

Know Your Enemy

I had another revelation while writing this chapter that has helped immensely in the area of forgiveness. Not necessarily a new concept in my life but one I had not fully applied to my family or my grandfather.

I've read 1 Peter 5:8 many times. It says, "Be alert and of sober mind. Your enemy the devil prowls around like a roaring lion looking for someone to devour" (NIV).

After working through my own hurt and need to forgive regarding my grandfather, I see the verse in a new light. Those words, *"Your enemy the devil"* hit home in the hurt places of my heart.

Through this verse, I realized no one in my family is the enemy. I am not saying that dealing with the relationships, boundaries, offenses, and the like do not matter, nor am I brushing aside the fact that there are consequences for negative behavior and actions.

However, we are called to reconciliation. In light of that, I am saying in the process of seeking personal restoration and healing and reconciliation with family, we need to realize that we are not truly fighting against the person in front of us. We are not fighting against the people in our past. We are ultimately fighting against one whose sole purpose is to destroy anything and everything that remotely points to our heavenly Father. When you see your family members and ancestors through the lens of Scripture, you won't be able to help but have some level of empathy and compassion. They are in the same battle you are, and they have been captured by the enemy. They are not *the* enemy.

This realization has helped me make great strides in the area of forgiveness. It has spurred me to pray even more fervently for freedom from the destructive elements of the past for my entire family, for protection from the things that have plagued my family line.

I pray for angel armies around every one of my children to keep the devouring lion at bay. It motivates me to learn more about my family history so I am fully aware of the potential ways we can be derailed and detoured generationally.

Charted Steps

Forgiveness and making amends are not easy subjects. Admitting you have hurt someone or confronting someone who has hurt you are both uncomfortable, vulnerable acts that go straight to the heart and soul. Both, however, are a necessary part of the process of living a godly life and creating the legacy imprint that will bless your family.

IMPRINT: Making Amends
IMPRINT: Forgiveness

I have only one step for you this time because I know how difficult it may be. Use wisdom, and prayerfully plan to make amends with someone you have hurt overtly or covertly, or someone who has hurt you if possible. Go before the Lord in private and ask Him for His guidance. Ask Him to show you what is in your heart before you take any other action.

If the person you need to make amends with is no longer living, use my letter as an example. Use the Empty Chair to help you heal. Write out the words you would say to them if they were here. Write about your experience so that those who come after you will be encouraged and spurred to forgiveness and growth in their own life!

CHAPTER 7

Finding Your Sea Legs

"For in every adult there dwells the child that was, and in every child there lies the adult that will be."

— JOHN CONNOLLY

'VE SPENT A LOT OF TIME ON THIS BACK PORCH recently, contemplating all that I am learning about my family. Realizing the long-term imprints in each of my ancestor's story and that I have become the "keeper of the story" opens a new dimension.

I feel as if a spotlight is shining down on me at this moment. I am in the eye of the storm, and a multitude of events swirling all around me have come together to bring me to exactly where I am in exactly this moment. I must now take on the role of weaving all the storylines together, including the overlapping moments from my parents' and mine, and add in my own — the major events, the ones that have shaped me and made me who I am. I must include those childhood moments that stand out as defining moments, that imprinted my life, shifted perspective, defined the fears, hopes and dreams, the humor and tragedy, the safe places, and the risks of my own life.

There are many tales I could share about my childhood years. In light of the legacy and imprints we carry, a few stand taller than the rest. Childhood is the time of our voyage when we get our sea legs. We learn the good and the bad about the world around us and develop our own ways of responding. When we are kids, our stories are intertwined with those who raise us. The impact of their story has the most direct imprint on our own out of any other in a generational line.

For the Mauck family, the actual story of my parents' courtship and marriage brings a bit of family drama that in hindsight and over time, allows for plenty of humor in the telling. To begin their story, however, I need to back up to a not-so-enjoyable time of my father's life, his service in the Korean War.

William "Louie" Mauck 1932– and Melonee D Nichols-Mauck 1935–
(My Parents)

William Louis Mauck, better known as Louie, served as an army corpsman. A childhood accident left him blind in one eye, ruling out a combat assignment, so Louie served as a field hospital nurse's assistant in the Korean War.

Toward the end of the war, Louie received orders to transfer to Tripler Hospital in Honolulu, Hawaii. Instead of field triage, he assisted the nurses in caring for the soldiers whose combat injuries warranted a trip back home — amputees, soldiers who lost vision or sight, the most severely wounded in the war. Unable to perform the most basic of daily tasks independently, Louie bathed, clothed, emptied bedpans, changed wound dressings, and fed those soldiers who could not feed themselves. The work was physically, emotionally, and mentally taxing.

The scars these wounded souls bore ran deep. The new reality some soldiers faced was so daunting and different, many could not cope. If injuries did not send them home, the thought of going back to what many considered hell on earth was unfathomable. Many attempted suicide, some more than once. Day after day, from sunup to sundown, Louie cared for these men.

Shortly before enlisting, Louie met a girl at church and married her after only a few dates. The young couple had little time together before he left for his tour of duty in Korea. Communication was sparse, and the distance in miles mirrored the gap that gradually grew between them relationally.

After transferring to Hawaii, Louie discovered his wife had been having an affair. When infidelity is uncovered in the army, you are given leave to "take care of things" at home. Distractions at home are distractions in the field and put soldiers at risk. It's understood the distraction will no longer be an issue when you return.

Louie returned home on special leave, but he was not welcomed with open arms. In fact, he was not welcomed at all. His wife would not see him, talk to him, or even let him into their trailer. Coming from a divorced home, Louie did not want to fail as he felt his father had. He wanted his marriage to work. However, every attempt to call or see his wife was ignored, making reconciliation virtually impossible. In the end, Louie reluctantly filed for divorce and returned to Hawaii.

A Fresh Start

By the age of twenty-three, Louie had seen the worst of pain and hopelessness in his time in the service. Still reeling from the loss of his marriage, Louie chose not to renew his enlistment in the army when the time came. He wanted a fresh start, a do-over of sorts. Needing a change of scenery, Louie left Hawaii, moved to be closer to his sister, Jolene, and her husband, Roland.

Jolene and Roland lived in Louisiana in the town of DeRidder, where Roland pastored the First Pentecostal Church. DeRidder was a Mayberry-esque kind of town, the kind of place where everyone knew each other, and everyone knew each other's business.

Louie immediately jumped into life in DeRidder. The first week he began studying music at McNeese State University in Lake Charles and immersing himself in church life at First Pentecostal, serving wherever needed.

That Wednesday evening, finishing up the weekly church dinner prep dishes and chatting with the rest of the kitchen crew, Louie watched folks arrive for Wednesday night service through the basement window. Three girls strolled by the window together, and one in particular caught his eye. Louie didn't know it then, but these were the Nichols Sisters. These sisters sang on the radio and in churches. Many thought of the group as local celebrities, comparable to The Andrews Sisters.

When he saw the youngest, Melonee Nichols, he blurted out, "I've just got to meet that girl!"

The entire kitchen crew stopped working briefly and stared at Louie. Realizing the thought had not stayed in his head and feeling the heat of embarrassment rising, Louie nervously attempted to laugh it off and dove back into making sure the dishes were immaculately clean.

Later that week, Louie arrived for orchestra rehearsal and made his way to the horn section. Coming to his seat, he looked up to see none other than Melonee Nichols, the sister who caught his eye on Wednesday, sitting in the horn section next to an open chair. Melonee was holding a trumpet, same as Louie.

And so it began. Louie and Melonee saw each other every week at rehearsal, spent time together chatting before, during, and after about life, school, really about everything. Any time they were at church, Louie and Melonee were together, talking and laughing.

"PADIDDLE!"

Over the next couple of months, Louie and Melonee continued to spend time together at church. Louie thought about asking Melonee out several times, but a flood of painful memories from his failed marriage rushed in any time he tried and drowned his courage. So, for now, he remained content with a growing friendship.

A church in a nearby town held a camp meeting in late fall each year, and a group of young adults from First Pentecostal decided to go. Louie volunteered to be the driver for the evening, seeing the perfect opportunity to spend time with Melonee outside of church without actually asking her out.

On the way back to DeRidder, someone suggested a game of padiddle to pass the time. In case you aren't familiar with the game, a "padiddle" is a car with only one working headlight. The first one to see it yells, "Padiddle!" and gets the point. At the end of the game, the person with the most points wins.

The game was quite intense with everyone leaning forward, straining to be the first to see what was coming in the distance and exclaim "Padiddle!" before anyone else, then playfully arguing over who actually did see it first. Louie, with Melonee seated next to him, all of a sudden had a brilliant, and slightly terrifying, idea.

"Alright, all. How about this? If I get the next padiddle, I get to kiss Melanie."

Uncomfortable silence.

After a few seconds, Melonee smiled slowly and said, "Alright, because that's NOT going to happen!"

The game kicked back in, every eye focused on the dark horizon, kibitzing back and forth about who was going to win, the girls banding together to help Melonee see the next one first.

"PADIDDLE!" Louie shouted, pointing and causing the car to swerve and everyone to jump in their seat.

Quickly regaining his composure and control of the car, a triumphant grin spread across his face. That night, even though he didn't score the most points in the game, Louie still won. He did indeed get to kiss Melonee, a little peck on the lips.

After church the next Sunday, Louie finally worked up the nerve to ask Melonee out on an official date for lunch and golfing, to which she emphatically agreed. Another small kiss at the end of that date before parting ways sealed the deal. Both knew they were meant to be together.

A Line in the Sand

Roland had not kept his brother-in-law Louie's recent divorce a secret from his congregation. He had done his best to balance rigid church doctrine with Christ-like compassion and family loyalty. The church's doctrine regarding the divorce, however, was clear-cut and strict. Divorce was an invisible scarlet letter Louie unwillingly bore. His presence was allowed, even embraced by the congregation, but some lines were not to be crossed.

Melonee's mother, Merta Mae Nichols, seemingly welcomed Louie's presence and involvement in the church. Even if she had an opinion about his situation, Merta Mae did not want to be unwelcoming, that is until she got wind of Louie and Melonee's date.

Marching straight into Roland's office, Merta Mae's mama bear emerged. "Pastor Gardner, I cannot believe you invited that, that, divorced brother-in-law of yours into our church. Worse yet, that you allowed him to date my daughter. Related or not, you should have seen the trouble coming."

Remaining calm, Roland gestured toward the chair opposite his desk, "Now Merta Mae, have a seat, and let's talk about this."

Undeterred, Merta Mae continued, "You should have made it perfectly clear that he was not to get involved with any of the girls in this church after being divorced just a year. How could you let this happen?"

Roland made another attempt. "Merta Mae, please, let's be reasona…"

Merta Mae interrupted, yelling and red faced. "My Melonee will not be a casualty of that man's wayward path. Shame on you, Pastor Garnder! Shame on you!"

Merta Mae ranted on for what felt like an eternity to Roland. In reality, just a few minutes passed. He had just about heard all he could take. Slowly, he stood and drew in a deep breath, but before he could utter a word of a verbal throwback, Merta Mae drew a line in the sand.

"You tell that brother-in-law of yours that I forbid him to see or speak to my Melonee again. I want Louie Mauck to leave this town immediately. Period. End of discussion."

Merta Mae turned to quickly storm out of the office. She grabbed the doorknob, intending to slam the door for emphasis, but checked herself, regained her composure, and instead quietly pulled the door closed behind her. She was, after all, a lady.

Pastor Roland slowly sank back into the leather of his chair, incredulous, not quite knowing what to do next. That night, he relayed Merta Mae's ultimatum to Louie, insisting that the relationship end for the benefit of all involved, including him.

I Can't Live If Living Is without You

In spite of the hard line taken by Merta Mae and Roland's discussion with Louie, Melonee and Louie still managed to see each other over the ensuing months, mostly at church. Every time Merta Mae learned of a rendezvous, even a simple conversation after services, explosive objections reverberated around town and in the church community, which especially concerned Roland. Dissention among church members over his own family did not promote healthy church life or job security.

After being apprised one too many times of Merta Mae's unsettling public tirades, Roland knew he had no choice. He needed to meet with Louie and Melonee and address the situation head on.

The meeting was short and did not go well. Roland quickly realized that lecturing logical reasoning was not winning. So, he switched tactics. Leaning on family loyalty, he said, "I know you two care for each other, but there are some, including your mom, Melonee, who have problems with a recently divorced man dating within our church."

He looked at his brother-in-law. "Because you're family, I was hoping there would be more acceptance, Louie."

Leaning forward in his chair, Roland folded his hands on the desk, pensively staring down at the open Bible in front of him, silently pleading for God to give him wisdom. The atmosphere in the room was thick. It was the saddest and most sincere Roland had ever seen Louie.

At last he broke the silence, gently yet resolutely stating, "I am sorry. Please understand the difficult situation I am in. The conflict you two are creating with not only with Melonee's mother, but also within the church must stop, and I see only one solution. If you are going to stay here in this church and live in my house, Louie, it's best for all involved, including the both of you, if you break off your relationship. Completely. Immediately. Please. I'm asking..."

Louie and Melonee sat silently staring at the floor. Roland felt for them both. It was the saddest he had ever seen his brother-in-law. After a long pause, Louie took Melonee by the hand, and the couple left the office deeply disheartened. Sitting in his car, Melonee finally broke the silence.

"Louie, both sides can't be right. And we can't be the reason for all of this conflict. That's not right, either."

"I know. There just has to be a way..."

"If there is, I don't see it," Melonee softly replied.

The truth was hard. Melonee loved her parents and hated seeing her mother so distraught. Louie loved his brother-in-law and his sister and didn't want to be the cause of strife between them or the reason Roland lost his job.

Both wanted to do the right thing, and the right thing right now seemed to be to break up.

Let's Get Hitched

Well, that separation lasted about a month.

Soon after the breakup, classes at McNeese let out for Christmas break, and Louie headed to Indiana to spend the holidays with his mother, hoping the time away might take his mind off life in

DeRidder and Melonee. Back on his old stomping grounds, he easily busied himself with family, festivities, and friends. But every celebration and happy moment brought a twinge of sadness and only solidified the truth that life without Melonee was no option. These were the memories, the times, the future he wanted to share with her.

Returning to DeRidder after the holidays, Louie wasted no time. He called on Melonee's close girlfriend, Billy Jack, who enthusiastically agreed to help arrange a secret meeting out of sight and off the beaten path in a small town not far from DeRidder along the Texas-Louisiana border.

When Melonee arrived, Louie laid it all on the line.

"Melonee, these past four months with you have been the best of my life. The last few weeks without you have been the worst. Every time I laughed, my first thought was wanting to share the joy with you. Every gathering, I found myself wishing you were there. You were my last thought at night and my first thought in the morning. I want that to be true for the rest of our lives. I want to spend the rest of my life making you happy. I love you…now and forever."

Getting down on one knee, he asked, "Melonee Nichols, will you marry me?"

Melonee's eye filled with tears as she wrapped her arms around him and breathed, "Yes!"

Louie wanted to elope right then, but Melonee needed a little time. Absolutely, spending the rest of her life with Louie was what she wanted. However, she was not yet quite ready to so boldly go against her parents' wishes.

Grabbing her hands, Louie reassured her, "Don't worry. I have a plan. Don't give up; just wait to hear from me. You *will* hear from me."

"Man and Wife"

The young couple endured two more weeks apart before Louie once again called on Billie Jack as well as his best buddy, Sidney Marcentel, to help set his plan in motion. Billy Jack pulled up to the bank where Melonee worked around noon on February 19th, 1955, and Melonee strolled out to the car, expecting to go somewhere for lunch.

As she opened the car door, a white flash from the back seat caught her eye. Sliding into the front seat, she closed the door and turned to see a wedding dress. Her heart skipped a beat.

Already knowing the answer, she flashed a quick questioning look to Billy Jack, who just sat there smiling. Hugging, crying, laughing, hugging again, no words were necessary as Billy Jack and Melonee drove down Main Street and out of town.

Louie and Sidney waited just outside of town for what seemed to be the longest hour of his life. Questions and doubts bounced around inside his head, "What if she doesn't show up? She thinks Billie Jack is picking her up for lunch. What if she feels blindsided and backs out?"

Just as he was about to drive himself crazy, Billie Jack's car pulled up with Melonee beaming in the passenger seat. Before the car came to a complete stop, Melonee flew out, and the two embraced. The troupe quickly loaded up Louie's bags and excitedly headed about an hour south to De Quincy where Sidney attended the United Pentecostal Church. Sidney had persuaded his pastor to marry Louie and Melonee and handled all the arrangements.

Meanwhile, back in DeRidder, Merta Mae received a call from the bank.

"Mrs. Nichols? We are just checking on Melonee. Have you heard from her? She hasn't returned from lunch, and it's been a few hours."

Concerned but also suspicious, Merta Mae called around everywhere to track down her young daughter. With each, "No ma'am, I haven't seen her," response, Merta Mae grew less suspicious and more livid.

When Louie, Melonee, and company arrived at the church in Dequincy, a young Pastor H.L. Bennett was expecting them and hastily ushered the group inside. Fifteen minutes later, standing at the altar with Sidney as best man and Billy Jack as maid of honor, Louie and Melonee said, "I do."

Just as the pastor pronounced, "husband and wife," the phone rang in his study just off the side of the sanctuary. Everyone froze. Knowing, panicked glances flashed between the members of the wedding party. Excusing himself, Pastor Bennett left and answered the phone.

"Good afternoon, Dequincy United Pentecostal Church. This is Pastor Bennett. How may I help you today?"

As Merta Mae peppered Pastor Bennett with question after question, trying to ascertain the whereabouts of her daughter, he leaned out of the office door, motioning for a quick exit through the foyer doors. As soon as the newlyweds were out of sight, he politely interrupted, "Why, yes, Sister Nichols, we just completed the ceremony, and unfortunately, the couple has already left the church."

The Wrath of Merta Mae

"On the warpath" is a mild phrase for Merta Mae's state of mind prior to that call. Phones across the town and county blew up with Merta Mae feverishly searching for clues as to her daughter's whereabouts. Merta Mae alerted the local police, questioned several local ministers, and interrogated all of Louie's and Melonee's friends in an attempt to track down her daughter.

By early evening, Merta Mae had alerted everyone she had known since birth to be on the lookout for Louie and Melonee. Exhausted and heartbroken, she sank onto the couch knowing the couple would now forever be known as Mr. and Mrs. William L. Mauck.

Realizing how worried Merta Mae must be and how protective she was when it came to her girls, Louie and Melonee had no doubt the police had been recruited by her mother to bring them home. Instead of returning to DeRidder, the couple continued west on the back roads of Louisiana, avoiding main roads and highways whenever possible.

After driving several hours, they arrived in Baton Rouge for the night. They stayed a few days, splurging the first night on a nice hotel, but moving to something less expensive afterward to save money.

Back home in DeRidder, Merta Mae was struggling to sort out her mixed feelings. She was angry at Louie for taking her baby girl. She was mad at Melonee for agreeing to go.

"How could Melonee do this to our family? If I ever get my hands on that Louie Mauck...," she ranted, and then worried, "Where on earth could they be?"

Ranting and raving eventually gave way to pacing and fretting, and in the end, resignation. "What's done is done," she said stiffly. "And I warned her. I told her if she left, it would end her relationship with the family."

A day or two passed with no sightings, leads, or any word from Melonee. So, as a mother, Merta Mae did the only logical thing to do under the circumstances. She invited friends and family to join her at the church that evening to pray.

When everyone arrived, Merta Mae did not seem to be praying like the others but lamenting the loss of her young daughter. Most described it as more of a wake for Melonee than a prayer meeting. The evening ended with Merta Mae still shaken and confused, thanking everyone for coming.

When word first got back to Melonee and Louie about how emotional Merta Mae appeared at the prayer meeting, it was obvious they had upset her. But seriously? Would she really act like Melonee had passed away?

A sad realization arrived with that story. Even though friends were accepting of the new couple, family in DeRidder would not be welcoming them home. With no money and no home to return to, honeymoon bliss faded, and harsh reality set it.

Louie made a few calls and finally found family friends who had a small apartment behind their home willing to take him and Melonee in until they got on their feet and could get a place on their own.

Going back to the Nichols' home could not be avoided entirely. Melonee needed her personal things from her parents' house. Louie had packed up all of his belongings the day of the elopement, but without advanced notice, Melonee had nothing but a wedding dress, a small overnight bag Billy Jack had pulled together for the occasion, and the clothes on her back. Not wanting to owe her parents anything, they agreed just to retrieve those things that Melonee had paid for on her own.

The couple arrived at the Nichols' home the next morning with mixed emotions. Merta Mae greeted them cooly at the door and staunchly refused to allow Louie past the porch.

Shaking and a bit nauseous, Melonee nervously attempted to talk her way into the house. Before stepping out of the way, Merta

Mae made sure it was understood: Louie was not welcome in her home, ever, and once Melonee walked out that front door, there was no coming back.

Melonee took her mother at her literal word, carrying her things from the bedroom to the front door, making a handoff to Louie, who then hauled the loads from the porch to the car. After several trips, Melonee gathered the last load and fought back the tears as she walked to the front door and stepped out onto the porch. Merta Mae closed the door behind her.

The temporary housing Louie arranged did not last long. Once word got out about where they were staying, Merta Mae made feelings known. Trying to avoid any added pressure for the host family, Melonee and Louie felt it best to leave and put some distance between themselves and DeRidder after that day.

Landing in Lake Charles, Louie continued pursuing his music studies, and Melonee found a job at the local bank. Lake Charles was close enough to keep a finger on the pulse of DeRidder, yet far enough away to not deal with icy rejection on a daily basis.

Icebreaker

It's been said that two things bring a family together — weddings and funerals. Well, not always weddings in my family's case! I add to that list as a general rule...grandbabies.

After my parents, Louie and Melonee, had been married about eighteen months, my older sister, Canda Lou Mauck, was born. Merta Mae heard of the birth of her first grandchild secondhand through the grapevine, and her heart began to soften. Having several grandchildren of my own, I can attest to the fact that grandbabies have the power to melt the hardest of hearts. With that softening came forgiveness followed by acceptance.

Realizing Louie and Melonee's love was not just some fleeting young romance destined to fade away, my Ma Maw and Pa Paw finally chose to end the standoff.

As soon as Ma Maw Merta Mae cradled Candy, her first grandbaby, in her arms, the miracle of love surrounded everyone in the room, and my parents and grandparents were never estranged again. In fact, my Ma Maw has been heard to say Louie Mauck is one of her favorite son-in-laws.

When my parents celebrated their sixty-third anniversary on February 19, 2018, I retold their story to my children and grandchildren that day. We laughed at the funny parts, cried at the hard things, and ate great food while celebrating this amazing couple and their story, a story sixty-three years and counting after one date and a controversial and highly protested elopement, a story full of imperfections with joy and laughter, hurt and sadness, woven with love and a theme of redemption, a real-life story I wouldn't trade for the most perfect love story in the world.

Robin Kent Mauck (1958–)
(More of My Story)

Two years after my sister Candy's birth melted the ice between my parents and grandparents, I came along. My given name is Robin Kent Mauck. My father named me "Robin" after the famed tale "Robin Hood," and my mom chose my middle name "Kent." My close friends and family call me Kenny.

My ancestral story began with Hans, moved through Frederick, Samuel, Joseph, "Wild Bill," my great-grandfather, Tom, my Grandfather Lewis, my father Louie, and now mine and my father's storylines intertwine. I carry with me not only the generational life imprints passed down from those who've gone before me, but also imprints made on me throughout my life, all of which I will pass down to the next generation of the Mauck family.

A Matter of Life and Breath

As a youngster, I had really, really severe asthma. The first three years of my life, my parents mastered "tag-team" nighttime parenting. I had to sleep sitting up so that I could breathe easily.

My parents took shifts throughout the night, one getting a few hours of sleep while the other sat up with me, then trading off. Not to get too scientific, but inhalers as we know them today did not become a standard treatment for asthma sufferers until the early to mid-1960's. Nebulizers were not nearly as effective, so unfortunately for my parents, and for me, I had little relief as a baby and even into my toddler years.

While my asthma was no joke, we all laugh now at the funny stories Mom and Dad share from those years, like the time Dad's cousin Paul and his friend Buddy came to visit. We were playing, and they started tossing me back and forth through the air, unaware that I even had asthma.

The three of us were having a grand ole' time until I started turning blue, which kind of freaked the two young single guys. My parents quickly intervened, reassuring everyone that I would be okay but also admonishing everyone to be more careful in the future.

For me, asthma attacks were like clockwork, a not-so-fun part of the evening routine for my family. Each one included an intense episode of croupy coughing and ended with me finally passing out to the hum of a large, oversized house fan and the aroma of Vicks VapoRub generously spread all over my chest.

Good times.

When I was about three, my family moved to South Bend, Indiana. After the events surrounding Mom and Dad's elopement, Uncle Roland resigned from First Pentecostal in DeRidder,

Louisiana, and accepted a pastorate at a church in South Bend. My dad's parents had separated, and my grandmother was now living in South Bend as well. So when my father's employer opened a new branch in the area, it made sense to transfer.

By then, my asthma had landed me in the hospital more than a few times and caused my mom to miss more Wednesday nights and Sunday services than she attended. One Sunday night in particular, I was having one of my worst episodes. My mother's concern grew as each breath became shallower, and the wheezing increased.

Dreading another trip to the emergency room, she called my uncle right before the start of service to ask for prayer. By the time he hung up the phone, the music minister had already started, but my uncle was so alarmed by my mother's call that he walked in, went straight to the podium, and raised his hand to stop the singing. Sharing his conversation with my mother, he asked everyone to stand with him and pray for me.

At the same time, at home, my mom began praying for God to touch my lungs and open my airways.

What happened next was nothing short of a miracle.

Within five minutes of those prayers, I drew in a long, deep breath. And then another. And another. The wheezing subsided. My breathing calmed, and the asthma attack suddenly ended.

I rested in my mom's arms as she held me and cried, thanking God for His mercies and goodness with each unhindered breath. When I finally fell asleep, she gently laid me down in my bed.

For the first night since my birth, my parents received the gift of a full night's sleep. I slept through the night until morning, and I have had not one episode of asthma since that evening.

Skeptics may attempt to explain my miracle in terms of scientific or medical reasoning, but I have searched and found little medical evidence to support the sudden curing of asthma. Some may call it coincidence, saying I just finally grew out of it, but for me, there really is no other explanation.

As a believer in Jesus Christ, I know I was healed. I experienced a real miracle.

Now, I don't understand why some people are healed and some are not. That's a theological question I'll let someone else tackle. What I do know is up until that night, I was a very sick little boy, and since that night, my sickness is gone.

While I no longer live with asthma, I still have emotional scars. I dealt with an enormous imprint of fear growing up, especially when it came to heights, deep water, and being alone.

Demo, a True Friend of Mind

An active imagination is essential to being a kid. Like most kids, I had a great one.

Remember those little green army men? I had a ton of them, and I'd set up battles and barracks all over the living room. The battles my armies fought were epic — bombs exploding everywhere, paratroopers floating through the air, cannons blasting enemy strongholds.

As a high-ranking general, I led my men into battle, chest out, knees high as I marched — BOOM! I would dive over the back of the couch in the wake of a massive detonation. Nothing made me madder than one of my sisters destroying rows of military organization as she shuffled her way from the bedroom to the kitchen, ruthlessly pulling me back from the battlefields of my mind into the reality that it was time for dinner.

As a hunter of great fame, I built my own hunting lodge in our backyard out of cardboard boxes and scrap wood and hunted the most magnificent birds of prey with my trusty Red Ryder. Colors carried feelings and emotions. I didn't just see black and white; I saw good and evil.

My imagination also comforted my fears. One of my many fears was being alone in my room. My sisters shared a room and had each other. Mom and Dad shared a room. I couldn't understand why I had no one.

Then one day, I met Demo. Demo was loyal, brave, fun, and a little mischievous and quickly became my best friend. We were inseparable. Whenever I needed someone to play with, Demo was available. If I needed someone to talk to, Demo dropped by. In fact, Demo did everything with me – played with me, sat with me when I didn't feel like playing, sang with me, blew up enemy soldiers with me, hunted game with me, ate meals with me, and slept next to me at night.

One morning at breakfast, I asked my mom for toast with my eggs and asked if my friend could have a piece of toast also. Without missing a beat, she asked, "What's your friend's name, Kenny?"

"My friend's name is Demo, and he wants toast, too, Mommy," I stated proudly.

Mom just smiled, nodded Demo's way, and said, "Nice to meet you, Demo," and placed two pieces of toast on the table.

Demo moved with us several times, but I finally lost touch with him somewhere between Portland and Vancouver. My imagination stayed with me, however. Over the years, my creative energies shifted from imaginary friends and make-believe war zones to writing songs to crafting articles for magazines and journaling inspirational ideas.

I give my mother a good part of the credit for the creative thread of my life. A holder of my childhood dreams, never once did she correct me or try to weaken my intensely imaginative mind, even though Demo did become a bit of a problem before we lost touch. Instead, she saw something special, something she believed God would one day use for His purposes, and somehow found a way to nurture and empower the good in it.

Bottoms Up

In 1964, our family moved from Vancouver to Joplin. Joplin is where I learned to ride bikes and horses. It's also where I became that great hunter of prey, wielding my first Red Ryder BB Gun. Yes, some of my fondest memories and one of my most valuable life lessons came from Joplin.

My first friend in Joplin, Mike, lived across the street. Those first few days, Mike was at our house all the time. We rode our bikes all over the neighborhood. He introduced me to the other kids on the block. Mike was about four years older than me, and I was flattered that he wanted to be my friend.

One afternoon, we pulled up into his driveway, and he invited me inside. His parents weren't home, but I didn't think it was a big deal since my house was right across the street, and my mom was home.

The front door opened revealing something I'd never seen before, at least not in a home. Mike's parents had built a huge wet bar right in the middle of their living room complete with glass shelves loaded with every kind of liquor known to man.

It was a hot summer day, and we were in desperate need of a drink. Bounding inside, Mike pointed to one of the modern, sleek, smooth leather barstools and said, "Have a seat!"

I hopped up, admiring the shiny, colorful display of bottles – short, fat liquor bottles, tall skinny wine bottles, beveled decanters – bottles of all sizes, shapes, and colors.

Mike slid behind the counter and grabbed some glasses. I was mesmerized by a shiny blue bottle on the far end of the shelf as I heard the glug of our refreshment filling the glasses.

"Wanna taste something?" Mike asked.

"Sure, I'll have some soda," I mumbled, still riveted on the blue bottle.

"Okay…" Mike laughed and slid a really teeny glass full of what did not look like soda in front of me.

I looked down and thought, *Wow, glasses sure are small in Missouri. I've never seen gold coke before.*

"What is it?" I asked.

"Just try it," he said, scooting the glass a little closer.

I hesitated, picked up the glass, and took a sniff. This didn't smell like any soda I'd ever had before, either. A little alarm went off somewhere in my six-year-old brain.

"Come on, just take a sip. It's not gonna' hurt ya," Mike urged.

I raised my glass, eyeing the golden liquid inside. Deep down, I knew I shouldn't, but I really wanted to impress my new friend. The alarm in my brain was fully audible now, but I quickly closed my eyes and tossed the golden liquid down the hatch before I lost my nerve.

"Fire, Fire! You're on fire!" my brain screamed. Instantaneously, I felt a searing pain in my throat, a hundred times worse than any sore throat I ever had. The inside of my nose was on fire. My eyes were on fire. Even my ears were on fire. I felt flames scorching my innards all the way down to my stomach. I looked down, half expecting to see myself actually burst into flames.

Letting out a piercing, girlish cry and sprinting for the door, I left as quickly as I had thrown that shot down, with Mike laughing at me all the way. Right then and there, I vowed never to drink straight whisky again (and I haven't to this day) and to end my friendship with Mike.

Mr. Oliver's Horses

When you move as much as I did growing up, lasting friendships are a bit of an anomaly. Uprooting and relocating during formative years can leave a child at a real relational disadvantage, making meaningful friendships somewhat elusive, which was probably why Demo stuck around so long.

Even if friendships were few and far between, my dad made sure we had plenty of great experiences growing up. One of them was thanks to Mike's neighbor, Mr. Oliver, who became a great friend of our family.

Mr. Oliver was a sweet man. In the afternoons, he would come out and talk to us when we came home from school and when my dad got home from work each evening. Dad and Mr. Oliver chatted about everything from the weather to the economy, but Mr. Oliver's face lit up when Dad talked about life on Grandpa Tom's farm.

The two would share stories, talk about farm life and horses and the good ole days. You see, Mr. Oliver owned a horse ranch near the Missouri-Arkansas border, and his favorite thing to talk about was his horses.

One evening, Mr. Oliver made Dad an offer he couldn't refuse. If Dad would bring us kids out a couple of weekends a month to care for the horses, muck the stalls, and make sure they had water and hay, Dad could teach us how to ride for free.

Dad jumped at the opportunity to pass on to his kids a way of life he had known and loved. So on weekends, my father drove us to spend Saturdays at the ranch. True to his word, in exchange for working on the ranch, mucking stalls, and putting out fresh straw and water, Mr. Oliver let us ride horses for free.

My horse was a lovable stinker named Lady, whose goal with every ride was to return back to the barn as fast as possible. Lady knew that once back at the barn, riding was done for the day. She looked for any opportunity to hightail it back to food and water. So my goal every Saturday was to get her out of the barn and keep her headed in the right direction on the trail.

I now live in an area surrounded by horse farms, much like Mr. Oliver's ranch and Grandpa Tom's farm. Daily as I drive home, I'm reminded of those horseback-riding days. I look back on Mr. Oliver as an angel of sorts for opening up his heart and sharing his resources with my dad, allowing him to create such amazing memories for my family, passing on a piece of family history.

Those childhood memories are precious to me. The work, the fun, the adventures, and the time spent with family are some of my fondest remembrances, memories that I, in turn, have passed down to my own family.

If there was horseback riding where we went on vacations with my kids, we were on the trail. More recently, I've taken my twin grandsons riding with me. I hope to instill a love and enjoyment of riding in them as my father did for me, passing on a family tradition that goes back generations.

My dad worked hard to provide experiences such as Mr. Oliver's horse farm for us. We also went on great family vacations. Vacations in the Louis Mauck family were a big deal, lasting more than a week and usually involving extended family. I remember one such vacation, not as much for the warm fuzzy memories, but the life lesson learned while playing with my cousins in the pool.

Fighting for My Life

When I was about ten years old, the entire family, including extended family, was tent camping at Carter Caves State Park, which happens to be not far from an area where Joseph Mauck lived with his family. My infant and toddler years struggling with asthma left an imprint of fear. When it came to swimming, that fear came screaming up out of the depths of my soul and yelled at me, "Water is bad!"

So it wasn't until that summer that I even attempted to venture into the deep end of a pool. Feet touching the bottom at all times was just fine, thank you very much. My twin ten-year-old cousins, Ronda and Jonda, on the other hand, swam like fish.

Watching my cousins splash each other, bobbing up and down in the water with ease in the camp's pool one day, I decided to carefully venture to the other side of the rope...you know, the rope that marks the slope down to the deep end of a pool. I grabbed the pool rope, gave myself a good pep talk, and bobbed under to the other side, death grip on the rope.

When I came up for air, I thought, *Hey, that wasn't half bad*, and bobbed back to the shallow side, never letting go of the rope. I did this a few times, not noticing the "sharks'" stealthy approach.

I surfaced on the deep side one last time. That's when I noticed them approaching, heads low to the water, sneaking stealthily toward their prey, one on one side and one on the other, closing in for the "kill."

And then in horror, I realized I had let go of the rope, which was now floating just out of reach. Before I could open my mouth in protest, I was under the water. Fighting to break free, I struggled to the surface attempting to gasp for air only to have the sharks pull me under again.

Instead of sucking in air, I was sucking in water. In what seems like slow motion now, I could feel their hands holding me under the water, hear them laughing up above me, taste the chlorine in my mouth, and felt the burn up my nose.

I could not breathe. Panic set in. A switch flipped. Somehow, I shot straight up out of the water, swinging wildly, landing a right hook square on my cousin Jonda's face. Another found its mark on Ronda, and she left the pool in tears. When I was finally able to get to the side, I climbed out. Angry words flew, and we all left the pool.

That incident at the time probably didn't seem to our parents like much more than kids being kids. I don't think for a minute they truly realized the level of panic nor the depths of the imprint of fear that years of asthma struggles had left. Honestly, I couldn't have articulated all of that at ten years old, either.

We all got a good "talking to," and I was punished for hitting my cousins. For me, I mark that as the day I realized in certain situations, you have to defend yourself. I also made a decision. From that day on, I would know how to swim. I am now an *excellent* swimmer as a result of this experience.

To this day, we laugh about the shark incident and many other escapades from our childhood. We reminisce about the good old days and about the shenanigans we would get into at their dad's church when my family came for a visit. So many great memories were made together.

The shark incident stands out because after it happened, I was different. I stood up for myself more after that day, and eventually, that developed into standing up for others. Since that day, I live with less fear. For that, I can thank Ronda and Jonda!

Home Sweet Home...Finally

My father's line of work impacted my childhood greatly. Working in the department store industry, my father made frequent trips to New York, sometimes as a buyer, sometimes for networking purposes.

I often dreaded his return from those trips because if we were moving again, that's when we found out. Too many times to count, he'd come back with a new promotion, and more often than not, that meant a new city.

The thought of packing up, starting all over at a new school, leaving our friends, and making new ones did not appeal to me at all. By the time I was eleven, we had lived in West Lake, Louisiana, South Bend, Indiana, Portland, Oregon, and Vancouver, Washington, Joplin, Missouri, Mobile, Alabama, and finally, Flint, Michigan.

When I was eleven years old, my father once again was offered a job with a better salary, and the family moved to Flint, Michigan. I remember my mother's first impressions of Flint. Driving through town for the first time, we all commented that Flint was not pretty. It was to us, in fact, ugly.

Turning to my dad, Mom said flatly, "Well, after this lovely tour of Flint, I have to say it's not the most beautiful place we've lived, which is probably why we'll end up staying here."

We all laughed, inwardly hoping Mom's words might come true. Why? We were all sick of moving! We had moved ten times in ten years and were ready to stay in one place and put some real roots down.

My mother's words were prophetic. When the company my father worked for closed its doors, instead of traveling to New York as he always did, my father teamed up with investors and opened his own store, Genesee Fabrics. I think he sensed a mutiny in the works if he attempted to uproot us again.

So, from fifth grade at Buffey Elementary until graduation from Kearsley High School, I went through more than one school year with the same group of friends and settled into a community. I called Flint home for more than twenty years.

Discovering My Calling

You've probably been asked before, what teacher do you remember the most? I would ask, "What teacher left the greatest imprint on you?"

In fifth grade, I met one such teacher, Mr. Walton. Every day at recess, Mr. Walton would supervise and somehow find the time to speak positive things into each one of our lives. He would commend sharing and good choices and recognize the strengths he saw in each child.

I remember one specific time I was running with some of my friends, and he called me over. "Hey, Kenny," he said, "you have a great stride. Have you ever thought about running track and doing field events for the school?"

The look on my face must have given away that I wasn't even sure what field events were, so he explained, "At the end of the year, we have field events that include relay races, sack races, sprints, and the long jump." Well, that sounded great to me, so I signed up for all four events.

I took home three blue ribbons.

Not only did Mr. Walton give me the confidence to try something new by affirming in me what I didn't see, but memories of his influence in my life also helped me decide to become a teacher. Not just any teacher, but I wanted to be the kind who found something to affirm and encourage in every student. I've carried that calling, modeled so well by Mr. Walton, into every career path I've been blessed to follow.

The influence of Mr. Walton was truly an early life-gift moment to me. He not only taught me to believe in myself and my abilities, he believed in me as well. He could see me doing great things, and running would be a part of it. Even to this day, I realize we all need a Mr. Walton in our lives to remind us what makes us unique and point us toward our purpose.

Hurdles on and off the Track

Elementary school was just the beginning of my career in track. Kearsley High School had one of the best track coaches around, Don Marsh. Coach Marsh inspired those who ran for him to do more than just attempt to be good; he expected and demanded the best from us.

Coach also had the gift of encouragement, and he had a knack for finding talent for his track program. Kearsley assistant coaches would attend middle school track meets to scout out the next generation of runners. I remember after one meet, one of the assistants, Coach Tiel, came up to me and told me to keep up the good work; Coach Marsh thought I had the potential to make a great addition to the Kearsley team one day. Those words motivated me all through junior high.

In my sophomore year, I finally began running for Coach Marsh. My main event was hurdles. I wasn't that good at first, continually knocking over too many hurdles. Coach always encouraged and believed in me, and gradually I improved.

My junior year, I started participating in more track meets but still struggled with knocking over that last hurdle. It wasn't until my senior year that I really found my stride.

We were undefeated in our meets that year and made it to the Big Nine Championship Meet. *Chariots of Fire* also came out that year, inspiring young runners around the world, myself included.

I prayed that I would run as unto the Lord, in true Eric Little fashion. I remember humming the chorus, "This is the day that the Lord hath made; I will rejoice and be glad in it," throughout the day. I ended up racing my all-time best in the 120-yard high hurdles that afternoon and set a new Kearsley High record in the 330 low hurdles.

While basking in the glory of my record-setting run and feeling pretty good about myself after the race, Coach Marsh came up to me. He put his arm around my shoulders and said, "Kenny, nobody will ever beat that record."

Wow, I thought. *Coach is really proud of me!* as a huge grin spread across my face.

With a twinkle in his eye, Coach went on, "You see, after this year, races will be measured in meters. So, technically, no one will ever beat your record because it's in yards." He always knew just the right way to remind us to be humble in our victory.

I still chuckle about that conversation. As far as I know, I do still hold that record. Of course, just as Coach said, the race has since been adjusted to 300 meters, so nobody will ever officially beat that record. Even so, I'll take the win, the record, and the sense of accomplishment.

I can only explain that day as feeling God's joy as I ran. The curse of falling on the last hurdle that had weakened my confidence and dampened my morale over the past few races was crushed that day. I knew He was with me as I sprinted that race in an almost out-of-body experience, feeling as if I was soaring over each hurdle.

Navigating Your Story

Just as it has for me, the process of discovering your ancestral stories and realizing the imprints made in their lives can give you a new perspective on your life. It may have already as you've read through the previous chapters and done the work at the end of each one. For me, I look back on these moments — my parents' story and the childhood memories that stand out in my mind with new clarity.

Time gives us the gift of hindsight, a chance to look back on situations with a bigger-picture perspective and hopefully greater wisdom. We are able to find the humor, such as in the story of my parents' courtship and elopement. Living it, I'm quite sure, was not fun, but since then, my parents and grandparents could chuckle when sharing their story.

We are better able to see patterns and themes not just in our own lives, but passed down from generation to generation when we take the time to look back. The overlaps of faith, risk, fear, forgiveness, loss, and lessons learned so much more rise up from the pages and strengthen our understanding of the why's of our makeup.

Running

One theme weaving its way through my family story is that of running, running from, running to, and actual running in my own story. Hans ran from persecution; Frederick ran in search of significance; Joseph ran to alcohol to escape his own personal demons; Uncle Tom ran to God for healing; Grandpa Lewis ran away from responsibility; and my father ran from the pain of an absentee father and failed marriage, also in search of significance.

The imprint of my father's running is the most felt for me. Bouncing around from town to town, between several states made it virtually impossible to develop deep friendships in my formative elementary school years. I was always "the new kid," the last one picked for team sports, the one trying to fit into the established clicks and hierarchy. It's probably a good explanation as to why I now root for the underdog. I don't like anyone to be left out because I can empathize.

A mobile childhood also impacted my life in that I made a decision early on that I would do things differently for my family. I committed to giving my children the opportunity to grow up in one place and establish deep roots, the kind I didn't get a chance to grow until high school.

One way of life is not right and the other wrong. That's not at all my point, but both make an imprint on those who live it out. Both ways of life have an impact that affects choices we make later in life.

Victory

Running left another imprint in my life. Reflecting on my track days and the imprints left by Coach Marsh and my experiences, I've drawn inspiration as I have faced hurdles in business and life. I'm reminded that just like that championship day in high school, God still champions me, picking me up, dusting me off when I fall, and carrying me over each hurdle onto the finish line. Only now, I realize more than ever, the race before us is an eternal one, just as Philippians 3:14 says, "And I press toward the mark for the prize of the high calling of God in Christ Jesus" (KJV).

Your calling, my promise, the path He has laid out before you and me is the race we run. Any obstacle that stands in our way ultimately stands in the way of the Almighty, which means if we let Him carry us, let Him steady us, the obstacle really doesn't stand a chance.

Let me go back to that scripture, Romans 5:8, that promises all things will work for good for those called according to His purposes. No matter what the obstacle is — no matter what the imprint is — ultimately, it will be worked for good, for His purposes. We overcome in victory because our God will have nothing less.

For me, Psalm 119:32 says it well. "I run in the path of your commands, for you have broadened my understanding" (NIV).

I am grateful for the new and deeper understanding I have of myself and my God through what He is revealing to me through this study of my and my family's story.

Charted Steps

When you think of the standout moments from your childhood, what word comes to mind? What lifelong impact was made? Those would be your imprint experiences.

Just a few of mine would be:

IMPRINT — Miracles — Hearing the Story of My Healing
   from Asthma
IMPRINT — Fear
IMPRINT — Overcoming Fear
IMPRINT — Overcoming Obstacles
IMPRINT — Searching for Significance
IMPRINT — Affirmation
IMPRINT — Lack of Opportunity to Plant Real Roots in
   Formative Years from Multiple Moves

I could list so many more from my own life, some of which we've discussed already in previous chapters. The point is, each person's childhood is rich with discoveries to be made of what shapes us and makes us who we are as adults. It's more important that you uncover your own.

1. Think of your childhood and those memories that stand out the most — the funny, the not-so-funny, both good *and* *bad*. What about those memories sticks with you? What word associations do you make with them? Take some time to write these things down.

2. What adult figure, child, or friend helped mold, influence, or affirm you growing up?

3. Looking at your answers to the above, what imprints from childhood do you need to overcome that have stifled, hampered, or held you back from living life to the fullest?

4. What imprints do you need to fully embrace and move forward in your life as you pursue your God-given calling and mission? Journal your declarations. How will you move forward in this new knowledge?

The Nichols gather together for this picture, with (left to right) Marce, Melonee, Marcus (Kenny's grandfather), Casiel, Merta Mae, and Wanda (DeRidder, Louisiana, 1943).

Kenny's great-great-grandparents, Jospeph and Sarah Mauck, have their picture taken in Moccasin Ben, Kentucky in 1850.

Tom Mauk, my great-grandfather, was a man who turned his life around by accepting Christ at a tent revival. Our family would finally turn back to God, not perfect yet one of honoring God and family again.

Rev. William "Lewis" Mauck (Kenny's grandfather) and his family pose for a picture. They are (left to right) his wife, Tessa Elizabeth, and his children William (Lou) Mauck and daughter, Jolene (Portsmouth, Ohio, ca. 1939).

The LifeCare Family Services staff is what makes it one of the premier children and family organizations in Tennessee.

(Left) Kenny would establish a high school record at Kearsley, with the assistance of Coach Marsh, in the 330-yard low hurdles event (1977). (Right) Kenny's high school track coach, Don Marsh, hall of famer and national high school runner-up coach, watches his athletes compete.

Louie and Melonee will be celebrating 64 years of marriage in 2019.

The family gathers to celebrate Louie and Melonee's 60th wedding anniversary.

My sisters, Candy (left) and Tammy (right), have been an inspiration that God has used to teach me about His love and grace.

Our three grandchildren, Easton, Gracelyn, and Cooper, have made huge imprints on Raye Ann's and my lives!

Our children and god child as youngsters. We agreed as a family to take Aleeya in and live with us during a time her family needed support.

Kelsey

Aleeya   Landon   Megan

Here are our three grown children, Landon, Megan, and Kelsey. Each has left a lifetime of impressions that neither words nor pictures could ever do justice.

Pastor L.H. Hardwick (center), his sermon, and his sons, Steven (left) and Mike (right), helped LifeCare become successful due to their early support.

Ernie and Ann Robertson, my father-in-law and mother-in-law, are shown here. Ernie was a significant help in starting LifeCare and was on our board.

Don Evans, Chairman of the Board, life mentor, and family friend for 48 years, poses with his family (left to right), Kerri, Barb, Don, and Kim.

The LifeCare Foundation Board of Directors, (left to right) Bill Campbell, Jeff Parris, Bruce Boder, Chairman Don Evan, Dan Finley, and Jim Carter, pose together with Raye and Kenny (center) for this group picture.

Raye and I celebrated our 35th wedding anniversary in Venice, Italy.

On our way to Italy, Raye and I visited Giessen Germany where Hans Peter Mauck left for America in the 1700s. It was an emotional day as we reflected on the fact that our Mauck story began in this very location.

CHAPTER 8

Discovery

"It takes courage to grow up and become who you really are."

— E. E. CUMMINGS

"**M**AN, I AM SO READY FOR THIS,**"** my friend Greg sighed, taking a huge bite out of the best hamburgers either of us had ever eaten. It seemed everything tasted better today. Colors were brighter, the air was cleaner...the world was good. Yes, this was the life.

Greg was one of the few childhood friends I had aside from Demo. We played in the church pews — or more accurately, under the church pews — as little boys. Family connections had kept us in proximity to each other over the years.

Now we were both out of high school and ready to take on the world together. Two young men on an adventure, we had just met up in West Virginia, to attend college away from the parental units.

"Yeah, this is gonna be great," I answered, dreaming about the awesomeness of adulthood that laid ahead as I slathered my fries in ketchup.

Of course, we had no real idea then what adulting really meant.

Life in the Fast Lane

Greg and I were headed to Huntington to live with my Uncle Roland and Aunt Jo who had moved there years ago from DeRidder, Louisiana. I recently discovered we were only about an hour from Portsmouth, Ohio, the city where my four-time great-grandfather, Samuel, had passed away.

We planned to take the remainder of the summer to get settled. Then I planned to attend Marshall University of "We Are Marshall" fame. The sting of that fateful plane crash was still palpable around the campus, giving a defining resilience that only added to the charm of a college town.

I couldn't wait to run for the track team as a "walk-on" in the fall. We plugged into the youth group at my uncle's church and started looking for jobs. To us, we were living the dream, working men living on our own (with my uncle and aunt) and surrounded by beautiful ladies (the youth from church). We had reached the pinnacle of adulting in our fresh-out-of-high-school minds.

Tradewell Grocery had a couple of job openings, and both Greg and I were hired on as baggers. Working with Greg was an adventure. He was just downright funny, and he made working the third shift more than enjoyable: dolley relay races, high-speed dolley runs down the aisles, shopping cart races, riding the conveyor belts, and midnight cooking experiments in the breakroom once all the work was done. We would always have things shipshape by morning, but oh, we had fun.

On the home front, as much as we appreciated the generosity of my aunt and uncle (and living rent-free), staying with them kept the freedom we truly longed for at bay. Being on our best behavior was, frankly, exhausting. So as soon as we could, we found our own place in town, closer to work life and Marshall. Many plans and schemes came to life while we laughed until we cried into the wee hours on the balcony of that apartment.

We had a simple domestic agreement. Greg agreed to cook if I would handle the cleanup. Sounded good to me; I hated cooking anyway. Since Greg was in charge of the cooking, I let him guide the grocery shopping. To keep an eye on expenses, Greg suggested we take full advantage of the specials at Tradewells. Again, sounded good to me.

That first month, Tradewells ran a special on the all-American favorite Kraft Macaroni & Cheese. Who doesn't love macaroni and cheese? It's the meal that pleases everyone from toddlers to Baby Boomers, right?

As much as I loved that Kraft comfort food (still do!), after three straight macaroni-and-cheese dinners — one with ham, one with sausage, and the next one with SPAM — I began to second-guess the goodness of going along with Greg's food choices. Apparently, Greg's cooking skills weren't much better than my own. So, we became well-acquainted with another American classic, the McDonald's down the street.

Great memories were made that summer hanging out, eating terribly unhealthy food, staying up as late as we wanted, and just being two young, naive, single guys in that downtown apartment.

However, our dreams of extended independence were cut short one night after work. I headed home, but Greg had a date and said he would be home later.

Exhausted from a long day and facing an early shift the next morning, I went straight for my bed. A pounding at the door woke me around two a.m. It was my cousin, Ronda.

Greg had been in a severe car accident involving a drunk driver and was in critical condition. I hadn't even realized he wasn't home yet. Ronda was so relieved to see me because rumor had it, I was in the car with Greg.

The next day, the gravity of the situation became clear. Greg's car was a mangled ball of metal and was completely totaled. Ronda and I went to the crash site and found the windshield wiper in the trees above the scene of the accident. Skid marks led to the spot where the drunk driver ran off the road into the ravine and revealed Greg's attempt to swerve out of his way. Broken glass was scattered everywhere.

Knowing it would take weeks, and more likely months, for Greg to recuperate from his injuries, his parents moved him home to Indiana. I could not afford our apartment on my own, and I had missed registering at Marshall anyway in lieu of enjoying our new-found freedom, perhaps a bit too much.

Greg's accident was a wake-up call, and I put the brakes on, moved back home as well, and refocused on the future.

Crossroads

My parents had moved across town over the summer, and as I pulled onto the street of their new house, I immediately fell in love with the neighborhood. The street was lined with beautiful tall trees and stately, well-kept Cape Cod style homes.

My parents house was a tri-level home with a screened-in porch. Dad's store was just around the corner from the neighborhood, and the local community college was only a short bike ride by way of forested, winding backroads.

As soon as I moved back home to Flint, I applied to and was accepted at Mott Community College. Before I knew it, two years had sailed by, and I had my associates degree in hand. Most of my classmates were headed straight to the University of Michigan in Flint with a clear picture of the next steps. Even though I had focused on school, I was no closer to knowing what I wanted to do with my life.

Back at Kearsley High School, I had been in the choir in addition to running track. I sang in several different performing choirs and ensembles. I loved music, still do, but when push came to shove, and the world of music and the world of track collided, I made a choice. I chose track. I don't know if I regretted that choice, but I didn't like having to make it, having to give up singing in high school. I still wonder what might have been had I chosen differently.

I also found myself at a crossroads in my faith as many do during their college years. I grew up in the church and had studied the Bible, but I found myself questioning a lot of things. So instead of going to UM, I took a detour to Jackson, Mississippi, to attend a small private seminary, Jackson College of Ministries, and study music.

When I left home for Jackson, I still didn't have answers or a clear picture. One semester? Two? Did I even really want to make music a career?

In some ways, I can see that I was following in the footsteps of my dad and Frederick, running, searching for...something. This fly-by-the-seat-of-my-pants decision, however, would become a very significant time in my life.

When God Shows Up

Musically, my piano instructor, Wayne Goodine, took my understanding of piano and my playing to a whole new level. I had learned how to play the piano by rote and had been writing songs and performing in church. Wayne helped hone those piano skills and showed me how to really enjoy playing an instrument with precision. I'm a better musician today because of his influence. I met many other great musicians and singers, some of whom became well-known artists in the church and gospel music.

More importantly, my spiritual life took a huge leap forward. My prayers while in Jackson were pleas for my life to make sense. I needed direction. I didn't just want a degree; I wanted to know who I was. I wanted purpose. I wanted God to show up and reveal Himself in my life.

I needed to know God was real. Much of my faith was built on my parents' understanding and experiences. I didn't just want the God of my parents; I wanted my own undeniable personal encounter with Him and experience of Him. I was on a journey to discover my faith for real for myself.

One night toward the end of the semester, I was alone in my room praying all of these things, the same things I had been praying all semester. Kneeling with my arms lifted toward heaven, weeping, I cried out, "God, if You're real, I need to know. I need to feel Your arms wrapped around me. Just, please, show me that You're there. I want You not just to be my Savior but Lord over my life, over the choices and decisions I make, over everything I do."

God did meet me that night. I felt completely wrapped in the arms of my heavenly Father, so much so, I was at complete peace and fell asleep right there on the floor. Never had I felt more peaceful or more content, realizing God was truly real. I knew now not only did God exist, but He also existed as someone I could walk with and talk to each day.

I had found what I was looking for, and it was time to go home.

Back in Flint, I continued my college career at the University of Michigan and began arranging for and directing the choir at Faith Tabernacle Church where my parents attended. I poured myself into writing. I collaborated with others on arrangements and took the choir to other churches to perform.

Eventually, I started a band and handed the choir over to my parents. I continued writing and arranging songs. My years at Faith were rich musically and spiritually, and I'll always cherish them for the spiritual depth and the lifelong connection to the Christian music community birthed in that season.

God's Call and God's Timing

Around the summer of my junior year at UM, my parents relocated to Nashville. I found a summer job in Lexington, Kentucky, and had planned to go my own way. However, my sister was going through a tough time personally. I decided, with a little push from my dad, to instead find a summer job in Nashville and live with my parents to be close to her and help however I could over the summer.

That extra push came in the form of a motorcycle we had purchased together while in Flint. Dad said I could ride it to work every day if I came to Nashville. Well, that kind of sealed the deal, seeing as I didn't have a car.

Every day, I rode my motorcycle down Old Hickory Boulevard from Bellevue to the grocery store I worked at in Brentwood. If you're from Nashville, you know what a beautiful drive that is through wooded hills and beautiful horse ranches. Every day, I would stall out in the same place. It became a morning ritual: Stall out. Wait. Try to kick-start. Wait longer for the light to come on. Hit the quick-start, and finally move on. It was here that God whispered to me every day, "Someday, you will come back here and raise a family."

I tucked those words away in my heart. Within a few months, I would be back in Flint. I believed wholeheartedly that I would and had every intention of coming back to Nashville to make it my permanent home right after graduation. But our timing is not always God's timing.

Kenny Mauck 1958– and Raye Ann Hills-Mauck 1958–

I seem to fall into that category of people where nothing goes smoothly, and often for someone looking in, my life can look a little bit like a sitcom. Meeting my Raye Ann would, unfortunately, follow suit. Maybe "unfortunate" is not the best word because I look back on that time with a sense of humor and thankfulness.

My style of dating was spur of the moment. For example, rather than call a few days beforehand, I would just ask a girl right after church if she'd like to grab a bite to eat. I didn't plan much beyond that when it came to dating. For the most part, this approach had worked pretty well for me...until I met Raye Ann Hill.

The Most Beautiful Girl!

It was the end of the summer 1982. I had just moved back to Flint, Michigan, from Nashville to complete my student teaching. I intended to graduate that fall from the University of Michigan and return to Nashville.

I had about $600 saved up to cover expenses while I completed my degree. Honestly, it was not a lot of money to stretch over five months of expenses, even for a twenty-four-year old living on ramen noodles and peanut butter. When you finally get to the student teaching part of earning your degree, you still aren't getting paid. You are free labor to a teacher for an entire semester. Fortunately, some dear friends offered me a rent-free bedroom in their home, which really helped make the most of the money I had.

My friend, Tim, and I picked up right where we had left off when I arrived back in Flint. I knew Tim from Faith Tabernacle Church, where we both attended for years before I left for Nashville. Getting back up to speed after my absence, I asked Tim what was new since I had left. Had anything changed? Anything interesting happen?

A huge smile spread across his face, and he said, "Oh, yeah, three new young ladies are attending the church. Really good-looking young ladies."

Well, what young man wouldn't be glad to hear that news? Even so, I wasn't looking for a relationship. I had a plan, and my plan was still focused on returning to Nashville after graduation and getting a job. If I didn't find a job right away, I was considering spending some time in the Peace Corps.

Sitting in my first service back at Faith Tabernacle, Tim plopped down next to me and said, "Guess what? All the new girls I was telling you about? They're singing in the choir today. I'll point them out to you."

After praise and worship and during the offering, Tim leaned over and pointed out the three new girls. The first was a pastor's daughter and very pretty. The second had a sweet smile and radiated joy. The third? She was the most beautiful young lady I had ever seen. I couldn't take my eyes off of her. Believe me, I tried two or three times, but she had captivated me.

Finally, I gathered my wits enough to ask Tim, "*Who* is *that*?"

Tom, seeing an opportunity to mess with me a little, smiled sheepishly and said, "Oh, that's Raye Ann, and you can't like her because I do!"

That broke my gaze. I turned and looked at Tim. He stared back with a twinkle in his eye. Tim was actually much younger than Raye Ann, so I was pretty sure he wasn't interested in her and was pulling my leg. I said, "Well, I would like to meet her after church anyway."

Tim shrugged and replied, "Okay, yeah, I think I can arrange that."

After the service, Tim motioned to Raye Ann, and she headed in our direction. I thought, *She's even more stunning up close than from a distance.*

As she drew nearer, I realized I was staring and quickly averted my eyes, pretending to be looking for someone else. When I looked back, there she was, right in front of me. I was standing face to face with one of the most beautiful creatures I had ever seen.

"Raye Ann," Tim said, "This is my friend, Kenny. He just moved back home from Nashville." Trying to keep my composure, I held out my hand cordially to shake hers and thought, *I definitely need to get to know Raye Ann while I am here.*

Strike One! Strike Two!

The next time I saw Raye Ann was Wednesday night after church. I had been working up the nerve to ask her if she would like to go and grab something to eat after church. Shaking inside, I asked as confidently and coolly as I could muster.

She looked at me sadly and said, "You know, I would consider it, but my clothes need to be done for work, and I wouldn't want you to just sit there, watching me work."

I felt my face get hot. "Okay, well we can do a rain check and meet another time."

As she walked away, I shook my head trying to sort out my thoughts. *My clothes need to be washed? That's actually worse than I need to wash my hair. Have I ever been turned down on a date because of dirty clothes?* The answer was an unequivocal no. Strike one.

I needed a little time to regroup, so I waited a week until the following Sunday to take another swing at it. Pumping myself up, I thought, *It's Sunday. She's single. So am I. We both have to eat. I'll just ask her to dinner, and we can get to know each other. Simple. Easy.*

I waited after the service, and my face lit up when I finally saw her. I was happy to see her and asked as casually as I could, "Hey, would you like to go to dinner with me this afternoon?" *Perfect,* I thought. *This is going to be great.*

No. Not perfect.

Sweetly, she responded, "Well, I would, but I promised my grandmother I would have dinner with her this afternoon."

I was stunned. She continued, "I really want to, but I need to keep my commitment to her."

I recovered enough to get her phone number at least so that I could call her later that week. This was definitely not a good sign, though. First trumped by the laundry, now sidelined by her grandmother. I was more than a little leery now, and yet, perhaps it *was* such short notice. Maybe she really did have plans with her grandmother. If that really was true, I was impressed, and it potentially spoke volumes about her character.

Always the optimist, I left the church that day thinking, *Wow, she's a young lady who keeps her commitments.*

By this time, I realized that if this was ever going to happen, I had better step up my game. I couldn't remember ever being turned down for a date twice in a row by the same girl, a very humbling place for me to be for sure.

My thoughts were still swirling. *Maybe she just doesn't want to go out with me.*

My ego limping just a bit, a few weeks went by before I attempted again. Mulling the whole situation over one day, I thought, *You know, Kenny, you have never really tried to plan something in advance with her. She does have a full-time job as an executive secretary at General Motors, so her schedule is already pretty full. So, this time maybe give her at least a few-days notice.*

Light bulb!

As luck would have it, Second Chapter of Acts, a Christian rock group from California, was playing near Michigan State. I had heard the lead singer sounded like Stevie Wonder, and that intrigued me. With both Raye Ann and I being musicians in the church, I thought I had found the perfect opportunity.

I thought, *I am going to give this one last shot. Come on, Kenny, let's go for it. If she says no again, no more calls, no more attempts. At least you tried. If it doesn't work this time, then it probably really was just not meant to be.*

After picking up the phone and hanging it back up three or four times, I finally went for it.

Full Count with Bases Loaded

The phone rang a couple of times, and I was quickly losing my nerve until I heard, "Hello?" on the other end.

My mind momentarily went blank, and I all could say was, "Raye Ann, this is Kenny Mauck from church." I waited, holding my breath, bracing myself.

"Well, hello there. I know your voice. I'm glad you called!"

Relief!

I wound up for the final pitch, "Well, good. I have some tickets to what I think will be a wonderful concert with a great Christian rock group from California this weekend, and I'd love to take you. If you say no, just know I will air guitar outside your apartment window, singing all night."

Yes, way to go, Kenny. Good one! I thought.

To my utter delight, she responded, "Well, actually I was just thinking about you, and yes, I would be very happy to go with you this weekend."

Yes, hit it out of the park!

God's Love Is True Love

That first date with Raye Ann went well. The concert was great.

On the way home, we talked about the show, music in general, and even sang a few songs from church together. Leading up to our date, God had been impressing a specific scripture on my heart. I kept repeating it over and over in my thoughts throughout the evening.

The scripture was Matthew 6:33, "But seek ye first the kingdom of God, and his righteousness; and all these things shall be added to you."

What were "these things"? I wondered.

When I went to call Raye Ann the next day, the same scripture came to mind. I felt the Lord guiding me, *Do this the right way, Kenny, My way, not yours.*

Instead of telling her all the reasons we should be together, all the things we had in common on that call, I listened. I shared with her how much I had enjoyed the evening with her, and I found out she had a great time as well.

After a few more dates, the relationship seemed to be growing, but I had to be sure we were on the same page about God's direction in our lives. One night while talking on the phone, I told her I was open to being really good friends if that's what God's intent was for us.

We talked a little more. Before hanging up, I said, "Hey, I have a scripture I want to share with you. It's something that's been on my heart for a while. It's from Matthew 6:33, 'Seek ye first the kingdom of God, and his righteousness...'"

Before I could finish, she interrupted, "'...and all these things shall be added unto you.' I was just reading the same passage before you called. I have it right here in front of me."

That call put God first in the relationship. Our friendship turned from just two people dating into two people committing to a more serious and deeper relationship. We were married a year later on August 13, 1983.

Now some thirty-five years later, it's obvious to me that God was seeking to knit our hearts together with Him first for the long haul. Our relationship has been tied to a much deeper anchor and purpose than we ever could have imagined then.

Over the years, we have been reminded again and again of the first time we shared this scripture. Some of those "other things" added to our lives have been our three beautiful children, our three grandchildren, a son-in-law, and all the future in-laws and grandchildren. God has also added great friends, new dreams, and two legacy faith-centered nonprofit and ministry opportunities.

To this day, Matthew 6:33 has been the mantel over our lives. Like all marriages, we have been tested. In those times, we realize just how important those marital vows are that we made to each other so many years ago.

The feelings meter of marriage can change, but love ultimately is a decision. When times get tough, and believe me they have, we have reminded each other of this scripture the Lord gave us so many years ago. It's helped us get our priorities back in order.

Looking back, I can see God truly wanted our relationship to initially blossom as friends by putting Christ Jesus first in our heart and lives.

Getting My Real Education

That same year, I graduated from the University of Michigan with my Bachelors of Science in Elementary Education and started substitute teaching to get my foot in the door of the school system in Flint. I was fortunate to be able to work with my lifetime mentor, Don Evans, who was a principal at one of the schools in town.

I had known Don since I was ten years old, and since I had no experience, substituting at his school was a valuable opportunity. One day I would be the math teacher, the next day the kindergarten teacher playing on the floor, the next day the music teacher, the gym teacher...you name it, I taught it.

In one of the larger schools in a low-income inner-city neighborhood, the teachers and students faced overwhelming issues. Behavioral problems, drugs, lack of respect, even gang activity was the daily norm.

It's a little humorous to me that so much time is spent learning and studying in preparation for a career when the real education begins once all that knowledge is actually put to work. There are just some things no class can adequately prepare you for. I had heard the term "combat pay" bouncing around the halls regarding inner-city schools but didn't fully understand until I was in one.

Over two years, I found myself in every situation you can think of — from confiscating a knife brought to school by a student to sitting on my seat littered with tacks to dealing with constant disrespectful attitudes and behavior in the classroom from students who were twice my size. What struck me most was that usually time after time, the perpetrators and initiators were the same group of kids, and most of them came from less-than-favorable home situations.

My heart grieved to see these students learning such poor behavior patterns at such young ages. Now, I see how the imprints they received at home directed their entire outlook on life and heavily impacted how they responded to everything.

Don ran his school differently than many of the other schools in that district. His teachers, students, and parents were taught respect, which was paramount and essential to the learning process and environment. He trained his teachers well, making sure we had good manipulative and tactical skills to help children with learning disabilities excel. Teachers in Don's school also learned positive and assertive classroom discipline techniques to foster a peaceful, productive atmosphere.

On a personal level, Don showed me what it would take to become a "master teacher" and encouraged me on that path. Although I did not substitute exclusively at his school, I was continually under his guidance. I not only gained valuable teaching experience, but looking back, I can also see how exponentially I matured under his mentorship.

Marco's Mark

My first job after graduating and completing my student teaching was back at my alma mater, Mott Community College, filling in for someone on a sabbatical in admissions. I worked about a year in that position until the employee I was covering for returned to work. I then took a private teaching job until another position in admissions became available.

I ended up being hired full-time in the Academic Development Center at Mott Community College, from which one of my most heartbreaking and unforgettable teachable moments came. As a counselor, part of my job was helping potential students wade through the admissions paperwork and get registered for classes. A particular Hispanic young man, we'll call him Marco, left a lasting imprint on me.

I had been working with Marco, getting him and his brother the necessary admissions and financial-aid paperwork completed. All that was left now was registering for classes. Unfortunately, he had missed two appointments with me to complete the process.

Our oldest daughter, Megan, was around twelve months old and was having an allergic reaction to a new formula our pediatrician had prescribed. After hours of uncontrollable crying, several calls to the doctor, and feeling utterly powerless to help her, I finally left Raye Ann with Megan and headed to the local pharmacy. I clutched a paper with the name of another soy-based brand of formula the doctor recommended over the phone.

No, I didn't just head to the pharmacy; I flew. The urgency and stress were radiating out of my body. Moms and dads of young ones who've had this problem, I know you can relate.

I arrived at the pharmacy, and I'm sure my car made a few squeals and screeches pulling into the lot and parking. I flew out of my car and sprinted to the sliding doors and slowed just enough to speed walk through the store until I found the baby aisle. Not even slowing, I grabbed the can off the shelf and was making a beeline for the checkout counter when out of nowhere, Marco appeared in front of me.

"Mr. Kenny, I must talk to you right now. Something awful has happened, and I don't know what to do," he pleaded.

Out of the corner of my eye, I saw the cashier listening in while checking out a few customers in front of me. I didn't have much time. I really, really, really needed to get back home with that formula. "Listen, Marco, my wife is home with our baby who is crying uncontrollably. I really don't have time to discuss this right now. Can you come in Monday first thing in the morning? I will make sure to clear room on my schedule for you to see me. I will do whatever I need to do to see you first."

Marco and I went back and forth for a bit, him insisting he needed to talk to me right then, me insisting I needed to head home as soon as I purchased the formula. Finally, he leaned in and whispered, "Oh, Mr. Kenny, you don't understand. I have contracted gonorrhea, and my wife doesn't know."

For a brief moment, I stopped and looked at Marco as he continued, "I have no one else to talk to. My family would never understand."

The cashier cleared her throat and snapped me back to my frenzied state of mind. "Marco," I said quickly, pulling out my wallet to pay the cashier, "I realize by looking at you how difficult this is, but I have to get this formula home to my screaming baby. Now I'm asking you to understand. I will connect you with the doctors you need, and we can help you with this and keep it a confidential matter. I can even meet you tomorrow. I just have to get back to my baby girl."

I gave him my number and asked for his. He was staying with friends and didn't want to give out the number. I told him to call me or to come in first thing Monday morning, and I left.

I felt horrible all weekend. I wanted to help Marco, but what could I have done differently?

When he didn't show up on Monday as I had encouraged him to do, I pulled out his information for his phone number. I was going to call even if his wife answered the phone. I just had an unsettled feeling about...everything.

His paperwork was incomplete. Then I remembered he had been in a hurry when filling it out and said he would finish it at the next appointment, which, as I said, he had missed. All week, I kept hoping he would come in.

Marco never did come to the office. On Friday of that week, I was informed by one of our staff members that he had taken his life.

I was devastated. I was a fledgling counselor, still in training. I had no idea he was so deeply distraught, that he would go to such lengths when I left him in the drugstore. Thoughts raced through my head — *Suicide? Why? How did I blow it? Why didn't he call? Didn't he understand my daughter was crying? I didn't see that coming. How could I not see it? How could I miss it?* I was twenty-eight years old.

That weekend at Marco's funeral, I was the only Mott staff member in attendance and the only one who knew about Marco's secret. I wept for his wife and small children as I sat in the back of the Catholic church, eyes fixed on the crucifix hanging high above the altar in the front of the church. Christ's arms were stretched wide in love to a world that unmercifully drove a spear in His side.

I was still in shock. *I had no idea Marco would take such a drastic measure. I didn't see it coming. I lost my only chance to help him. What could I have done differently?* I carried the hurt and pain from Marco's death with me for years.

It wasn't until several years later that I realized what that something I could have done differently was. In my post-graduate masters in counseling studies, one of the first course electives was a class on recognizing the signs of someone at risk of committing suicide. I learned the differences in behavior between a person just thinking about following through and someone who actually has a plan in place.

In that class, I realized that instead of trying to console and redirect Marco, I should have been asking the right questions, finding out if he was thinking of hurting himself, discerning if he had a plan. I realize now I was too young and inexperienced to see the signs.

Over the years, my experience with Marco has saved many people. I am so thankful to my Lord that in the twenty-plus years since then, I have never lost an individual I have counseled. That's not to toot my own horn or to say it will never happen. I sincerely hope it never does. But if by learning from mistakes made with Marco, I can help someone see that life is a gift, help them discover the plethora of reasons they have to live, laugh, and love each day, that the problem is temporary, and there is hope, then his loss is redeemed, even if just a little.

The Revolving Dollar

While working in the Academic Development Center, I had the opportunity to be a counselor for a grant program entitled "College Survival Skills." The program targeted single-parent adult students who struggled to succeed academically for a variety of reasons. These particular students were given a second chance and the assistance needed to obtain their two-year degree. Many of these parents struggled to stay above the poverty level. Not only did they struggle with the academic side, lack of a support system to help with childcare hindered their ability to attend classes.

Both of those issues were solvable, for the most part, through government aided programs and offerings through the college. One last obstacle was sometimes the most difficult, though, as seemingly small as it might be to the average person. Bus fare. Some of these single parents just did not have the one-dollar bus fare each way left in the budget after covering everything else.

My heart broke for these parents who were working so hard to make a better life for themselves and their children, only to be stopped dead in their tracks for want of a dollar. At first, I pulled money out of my own wallet to help out, but working with so many students, I began to feel the pinch in my own budget. These students didn't want to have to borrow money from me, and I was not sure if I could continue this financially over the long road either.

Laboring over this issue one day, it came to me. I contacted my caseload of single parents with my idea of the Revolving Dollar. I would start by hanging up the first one-dollar bill on my billboard in my office. If someone needed bus fare and took it down, it had to be replaced the next day by them or a fellow classmate. If you took the dollar, it was your responsibility to reciprocate with a dollar as soon as possible. If you noticed the dollar was missing and had a dollar to give, pin it up there.

Being a part of empowering someone to achieve their dreams without doing it for them is something everyone needs to experience. A day never passed where the dollar wasn't used, nor did a day ever pass where the dollar wasn't replaced.

Sometimes, more than one-dollar bill was on the board. To me, single parents are heroes, especially these. They worked so hard and took advantage not of a handout, but of a solution to a problem and an opportunity to give and receive. They ran with it in pursuit of their dreams of finishing college.

I carry that revolving dollar mentality with me still into other areas of my life. It's why I had money in my pocket when I said goodbye to Carlos and bought him a snack from the vending machine. I make sure I have a dollar or at least change in my pocket whenever I go to one of our centers.

I've seen the impact a single dollar and a simple act of kindness can make, the empowerment it can give. Sometimes showing love in the most practical, simple way *is* feeding a soul and sharing the love of Christ.

Navigating Your Story

The time between childhood and adulthood — adolescence and young adulthood — is a beautiful, treacherous, gut-wrenching yet amazing season of becoming and discovery. We begin to explore and discover who we really are outside of our parents' influence. We find and develop for ourselves our faith and beliefs.

The search for purpose and the answer to the question, *Why am I here?* come to the forefront. This is the leg of the voyage when we begin to take ownership of our journey, make decisions on where our ship is going, try to figure out how it will get there, and determine who we want along for the ride.

Young adulthood is where blinders are removed. Rose-colored glasses fall off. As children, we are the center of our universe, and we filter life through that lens. As we move from childhood into our twenties and even thirties, we begin to see that we are part of something much bigger than ourselves. It's not the first time we've heard of the bigger picture, but for many, it's the first time we actually see a bigger picture.

A Matter of Trust

This season of discovering who I was, of discovering my own relationship with the Lord, prepared me for what was ahead, for the greater work that would become LifeCare. But eight years passed between my time at Mott until that epiphany moment mowing my lawn back in chapter five.

Eight. Years.

Eight years of waiting. Eight years of questioning. Eight years of arguing. Eight years of sometimes burying my head in the sand.

Doubt wasn't the issue. I didn't doubt that God existed or had spoken to me. I believed I was supposed to go to Nashville. I believed *He told me* I was supposed to go to Nashville. So, why didn't I just jump in headfirst right away and go?

Trust.

Believing I heard Him was not enough. Believing in Him was not enough. Believing He had it all figured out and had the answers, now that was another story.

Trusting that He was going to make it all happen, take care of me, have a job for me so that I could support my family? Trusting that friendships were waiting for me, that purpose was waiting for me? Giving up the life Raye and I were building in Flint, the friends and family, the security and comfort we had? Pulling up the roots we had set?

I couldn't actually see that part. Roots were a big deal to me now that I had control of my own life and movements. Pulling them up scared me. I had things figured out and under control in Flint, and I liked it that way.

I firmly believe God's timing is perfect. I had taken baby trust steps along the way, but at this point in my life, this looked like a record-setting long jump of trust. It was a tremendous step for me, and His timing allowed for the waiting. Only in this instance, I wasn't waiting on God. He was waiting on me.

I'm reminded of Proverbs 3:5-6, "Trust in the LORD with all thine heart; and lean not unto thine own understanding. In all thy ways acknowledge him, and he shall direct thy paths" (KJV). Today, I can say He did exactly what He promised in these verses. He directed my paths. He has been faithful in every area. I could not have imagined the life we have, the plans He had for me, the company He would give me to steward, or the people He would bring into my life when I finally chose to trust Him with our future.

Charted Steps

IMPRINT – God's Revelation
IMPRINT – Finding Love
IMPRINT – Trust

Trusting God is an issue for many of us. Not trusting Him with relationships, with finding love, with our future, with our finances, with...*you fill in the blank* can put a roadblock in your journey to finding and fulfilling a purpose, to hearing His calling in your life. Identifying and working through any trust issues free us to walk confidently in God's purpose for our lives.

1. When you hear the word "trust," what emotions surface? What areas of life come to mind? Finances? Relationships? Future?

2. What about those areas is a struggle when it comes to trusting Him? Be as specific and honest as possible.

3. Spend some time praying over these things and asking the Lord to show you how they may be standing in the way of fulfilling your mission and purpose. Ask Him for help to overcome the need to control, your fears, whatever it is that keeps you from trusting Him.

CHAPTER 9

Assembling Your Crew

"Don't just find people.
Find your people."

— KENNY MAUCK

L EAVING A POWERFUL LIFE IMPRINT and legacy involves passion. Our company, LifeCare, birthed from a promise to Carlos that grew into a God-given vision and a desire to serve the underserved in our community will be a tangible piece of that legacy imprint.

I say "our" company because I did not do this alone. God has graciously brought people into my life to fill specific roles, guiding the process of building the vision. I'm surrounded by men and women who share a similar passion and who enthusiastically bring their skills and talents to the table in support of the vision.

The Crew

Choosing the right crew is important. Remember my original mission statement back in chapter 2, the one with all the positions I knew I'd need, the one with a blank space next to each job title? If I had just pulled that out, put together the standard job description, and started collecting and reviewing resumes and hiring based solely on that criteria, the LifeCare leadership in place today would most likely not have been chosen.

Even though I did post job listings and sort through many resumes, many times I did not hire the one most qualified on paper. Every one of my hires won me over during the interview or through a life lived before becoming an employee. Some are now dear friends and neighbors whose character and skills I had the opportunity to observe firsthand. All proved to be some of the most outstanding leaders and faithful workers I have ever had the privilege to work with.

Rule number one: Don't just find people. Find your people.

Don't exempt anyone based merely on a resume. Raw talent, gifting, chemistry, and passion are far more paramount to drive the mission. Be open to whomever the Lord puts in front of you. If you are hearing a "Yes!" in your spirit, even when the paper in front of you says, "No," listen to the voice. Don't just read the words.

My initial administrative and clinical staff consisted of a bus driver, a neighbor with triplets, a former college basketball player, a woman with a huge heart full of love for kids, a former music-industry employee, a conservative nurse from California, a community-oriented true country gal, a spouse with great attention to detail, a son with good people skills, and an auditor from another company who impressed me so much as a person, I convinced him to come work for me.

One of the first employees I hired was a young, intelligent Christian man named Sean McPherson. When I interviewed Sean, I had three job openings I needed to fill. At the time, Sean drove buses for a company that took students on trips to Washington, D.C. He had worked with kids in the inner city and as a youth group leader at his church while earning his master's degree. Outside of that, though, he hadn't had much opportunity to gain experience.

By the end of his interview, even though his resume said otherwise, I realized he was actually qualified for all three open positions. So, rather than choose for him, I laid all three options out and let him decide.

Sean went for the job with the most responsibility, and that spoke volumes to me. Over the years, I've grown to respect Sean as a man of wisdom and character. He's someone I have come to think of as a second son. He has been with LifeCare for sixteen years, became our vice president in 2010, and is positioned to become the next President of LifeCare Family Services in the fall of 2018.

Another one of my key leaders is Jim Carter. To this day, I can say I have never really looked at Jim's resume. Prior to his hiring, I already knew exactly what he did. I was aware of his reputation for excellence both in the field of mental health and administration and of his experience caring for handicapped individuals.

Jim became one of our clinical and administrative auditors. His keen eye and attention to detail are impeccable. Quality control takes time to develop and maintain and was initially a problem for our company. Then Jim came onboard, and under his leadership, quality control is now a defining factor of our company. Jim brought in "best practices" techniques to better serve our families, children, seniors, and those in need of rehabilitative services.

Jim has faithfully served over a decade, becoming vice president in 2011, and now oversees the daily operations of our sister company,

LifeCare Foundations. Foundations serves veterans, seniors, and people of all ages with a physical handicap or intellectual disability in need of 24-7 housing or adult daycare assistance.

I continued the unorthodox methods of hiring when I brought one of my neighbors onboard. I didn't notice her for an outstanding interview or stellar resume. No, she was hired based on her ability to multitask. You see, this neighbor is the mother of three children — triplets, who were babies at the time. I was always impressed with her ability to change three diapers and serve up three bottles all at once, utilizing only two hands and sometimes a foot. My decision to offer her a job was finalized one day while observing her through our living room window, putting the three kids into their car seats without shedding a single tear...her or the kids.

There's something to be said for getting to know your neighbors. Mine were very instrumental in the initial staffing of Lifecare. In addition to my mother-of-three multi-tasking phenomenal neighbor, I also hired Christy Scruggs based on the referral of another neighbor.

Christy played point guard on the women's basketball team for Middle Tennessee State University. Her time-management skills and ability to know when to delegate or take the task on herself have been a considerable asset to LifeCare. Having little billing experience, Christy came onboard and has grown into a great leader and a specialist in every aspect of detailed claims and billing.

Christy is a multi-talented individual who can do (and has done) just about anything put in front of her. She has been with us for fifteen years and is now Director of Claims with 3LS, overseeing the claims of both LifeCare and another subsidiary company, Omni Community Health.

Before any of these wonderful people came onboard, I hired Dominique Miller. Dominique's passion is at-risk children, and her contribution was essential at the beginning of LifeCare. Dominique managed our first advocacy cases, tracking progress and ensuring that kids who were struggling in school due to a poor home environment were succeeding after our involvement. The situations these kids lived in ranged from parents who abused drugs to neglect to physical or sexual abuse. Part of Dominique's work was finding a safe home with a relative, or in cases other than abuse, working with the biological parents to ensure the child thrived and could remain in their home.

Dominique recently earned her master's in social work and will be leaving LifeCare after twenty years of service for a new ministry opportunity with her husband. The indelible imprint she leaves behind covers my family, our company, and the hundreds upon hundreds of families she served.

One of the greatest stories of her impact on others I can share comes from one of her cases. A teenager whose case Dominique managed for years became pregnant, and when it came time to deliver, asked Dominique to be the one at her side. Dominique, being the passionate caregiver she is, absolutely agreed. As the baby was born, through tears of joy, the teen mother whispered, "Meet your new godchild. Her name is *Dominique!*" Dominique, you will be greatly missed!

Our head coordinating nurse, Rebecca Rahman, has been with us for eight years. Rebecca is a hoot. A California transplant and converted Tennessee football fan, Rebecca is without a doubt a true lover of people from any and every walk of life. With a background in insurance, Rebecca oversees LifeCare and Omni Community Health's medical coordination for the entire state of Tennessee. She's become a part of the family, even spending time looking in on and caring for my parents when they lived in Tennessee. A genuine person and faithful friend, Rebecca would be an asset to any company team.

One of our longest-standing medical providers is Tory Woodard. Tory exudes a genuine love for every person he comes in contact with regardless of status or background. An exemplary leader, Tory has been with us ten years and is one of the best prescribing nurse practitioners I have ever known.

Christal Wise hails from Lawrenceburg, Tennessee, a small city where the Amish still come to shop by horse and buggy and where most of the town know each other. Her knowledge of the people, the schools, the criminal justice facilities, and local businesses in the area make Christal a perfect choice to be our a dvocate in her hometown. She is one of the most graciously kind individuals you will ever meet, making it easy for those with whom she works within the system and the families she assists to be at ease and trust her guidance.

Myrna Kemp is another excellent addition to our leadership team. Myrna was one of the exceptions to my unusual hire trend in that her resume and experience exactly matched her position. She brings a strong work ethic and top-notch listening skills, both as a therapist and as a leader in the company. But Myrna's smile is what wins us all over. When things aren't going as smoothly as we would like at one of our community mental health centers, her positive energy and leadership are refreshing to all involved.

Like the rest of us at LifeCare, no job is beneath her. She willingly rolls up her sleeves and gets to the business at hand, and that's why she so respected by the team.

David Thomas rounds out our leadership staff. David began his career in Nashville in the music business but soon found his real passion and gifting were in counseling. David came to LifeCare from Cumberland Heights with experience in drug and alcohol recovery and has been with us for fourteen years. Starting in a licensed counselor capacity, David has grown with the company, finishing his doctorate in counseling psychology and becoming our Clinical Director a few years back.

More important than his impressive scholastic and postgraduate achievements, David is one of the most faithful, committed, and trusting individuals I know. His love for Christ is reflected in the way he treats his clients and employees. One of the most respected leaders in our organization, he illustrates with his life and work how a genuinely committed team member looks and acts at LifeCare.

The secret of LifeCare's success lies not solely within me as a visionary leader, but in the great people, like those mentioned above, who God has brought my way. Many have carried the vision and made LifeCare what it is today (and many more are listed in the back of this book.)

I'm grateful to each and every employee that has served over the last twenty-plus years. A vision can only go so far with one person. A vision carried by many has no limits.

Flying with Eagles

By mid-2001, LifeCare had completely overrun our dining area and our garage. After taking on our first few employees, we desperately needed more room. I began looking at options, but I wasn't sure our budget could handle the expense of outside office space.

At the same time, my friend Dave Ramsey was on the rise, shooting from local to national and even international fame as America's personal finance guru, both on the radio and through his Financial Peace University course. Dave heard I was looking to expand and graciously offered to sublease space to us in his offices at the Ramsey Building. Raye Ann and I gladly took him up on his offer and reclaimed our home and my wife's parking spot!

Early every Wednesday morning, Dave met with a group called the Eagles. The group consisted of ten to twelve men, all entrepreneur-types, great thinkers and leaders in the community, including a builder, writer, music producer, minister, marriage ministry founder, podcaster, speaker, men's coach and facilitator, CPA, commercial real estate owner and businessman, and Dave. Dave invited me along one day, and I started attending regularly. Those men and our Wednesday morning meetings became an integral part of my development as a leader and as a man.

Throughout our years together, the Eagles became more than just a bunch of guys in a weekly meeting. We became friends. We did life together. Every man in that group experienced extreme business or personal hardship or loss, including me. We prayed for each other, encouraged each other, read and studied great books together, such as *Mere Christianity* by C.S. Lewis and *Soul Survivor* by Philip Yancey. Our families spent time together. We attended each other's kids' weddings.

When our friend and fellow Eagle, Pastor David Foster, suddenly passed away, we stood with and supported his family — our family. Looking down the aisle at his funeral, I was so proud to see all of us, his fellow Eagles, celebrating his life together.

As LifeCare continued to grow, so did the demands on my schedule. Staff meetings, board meetings, meetings with accountants, auditors, attorneys, contracting, and staffing filled my day to the brim, and one of my biggest disappointments was not being able to make every Eagles meeting each week. Along with that, living so far from the Ramsey building only added to the stress.

Dave and the others were beginning to experience similar life and work demands pulling for their attention. Around 2012, the Eagles mutually decided it was time to disband, at least from weekly meetings. But that decade together bonded us deeply for life, and I know without a doubt, if I were to call any of these men today in need of real help, or if they called on me, we would be there for each other in a heartbeat.

Rule number two: Find your Eagles.

We need the accountability, encouragement, and support of each other more than we realize. For me, the Eagles became a tangible example of Proverbs 27:17, which says, "As iron sharpens iron, so one person sharpens another" (NIV).

We may convince ourselves that we are not relationally oriented or that we are fine with being a loner or "an island," but scripturally and practically, that doesn't hold water. For your ship to stay sound and seaworthy, you need a strong crew. You need people who will lift you up when you need it, challenge you, encourage you, and just do life with you. You need your own Eagles.

A Perfect Storm and a Perfect Gift

In 2009, the perfect storm hit our company. One of our contractors was beyond past due in payments, and we were bleeding over $100,000 a month.

After several months of trying to recoup the loss to no avail, we were forced to lay off one-third of our staff. Our little five loaves and two fish company had miraculously exploded to 200 employees with millions of dollars in contracts. Now, seven years later, to lose 1.75 million dollars and sixty great employees was extremely difficult to take.

We were broke, so broke, I asked all the remaining administrative staff, including myself, to take substantial salary cuts so that we could stay afloat. I put a freeze on purchase orders of any kind and cut everything else I could to the bone. Adding insult to injury, that same contractor, one of our largest, terminated our future contract. I went into a state of depression.

How bad were things, really? Well, Dave and his wife, Sharon, asked if I had any materials on losing a pet for kids. The family dog had died, and the kids were taking it hard. Of course, I did know of the perfect book, a therapeutic coloring book designed to help kids process loss.

When I went to get the book to give them later that week, I discovered a child had already started coloring in marker on a couple of pages. I literally had that one copy left. Due to my own edict forbidding the ordering of any materials until we got our budget under control, I could not order additional copies.

I had no other option. Using liquid white out, I covered the two or three magic marker spots.

I met Dave later that day and gave him the little bereavement book and apologized all over myself for its horrible condition. Two weeks later, I received a package in the mail. I was a little surprised because, well, I hadn't approved any purchase orders.

When I opened the box, brand-new coloring books spilled out onto my desk and sat there staring me in the face, the exact same one I had given to Dave for his kids. My eyes filled with tears.

Dave and I have never spoken about his gift. Even now, I get a lump in my throat thinking of his genuine kindness. I'm still touched and humbled. Dave absolutely saw not only my need but my unspoken desperation and threw me a life preserver. What might look like a seemingly small act of generosity to others spoke volumes to me of his belief in me and the value of our friendship. It gave me more hope than I think he ever knew. (Thank you, my friend!)

The Ramsey's remain great friends of ours. Our families have made some great memories together since our Eagle days, including many a summer on Tims Ford Lake here in Tennessee. Dave is quite the water skier and actually taught our kids how to ski out on Percy Priest Lake. In fact, it was Dave who taught not just my kids, but all of the Eagles' kids how to ski.

Safety in Numbers

One of the best kept secrets of our company is our board of directors, who serve as counsel to me both professionally and personally. I am fortunate to have great men and women serve on the LifeCare board.

God is faithful to bring individuals with the expertise I did not have to join in accomplishing His purposes for LifeCare. The diverse gifting and skills of those who serve have saved me from tumbling over a few dangerous cliffs due to lack of experience in many areas.

Each one brings so much more to my life than just business savvy and experience. I view them a lot like the elders or deacons in a church. I'm reminded of Proverbs 11:14, "Where there is no counsel, the people fall; but in the multitude of counselors there is safety" (MEV).

These people were and are spiritual leaders, wise counsel, and accountability for the LifeCare family of companies, and in many cases, me personally.

Don Evans
Chairman of the Board
Life Coach and Mentor, LifeCare Foundations
Board of Directors for Family Services
Visionary and Servant Leader

Don and his wife, Barb, have known me since I was ten years old when our families first met in Flint, Michigan. As a mentor and second father figure in my life over the last fifty years, he has been a gracious, unofficial life coach to me. Imprints of service, honesty, God, and family-first have been left on me simply by watching my friend live his life for Jesus.

One of his greatest attributes is having a servant's heart. Don would give you the shirt off of his back if he thought you needed it. No act of service is too small, including quietly coming over and cleaning out our rain gutters and trimming hedges when I didn't have the time.

He's been known to take care of a task and never say a word about it later. Without a doubt, Don Evans continues to be one of the most giving men I have ever met and is a phenomenal chairman of the board.

Bill Campbell
Board Member, LifeCare Family Services
Business Life Coach and Entrepreneur
Mediator, Collaborator, and Man of High Integrity, Wisdom, and Foresight

I've known Bill and his wife, Kathy, for over twenty-five years. Bill joined the board of directors in 2010, and has served as our chairman since 2013. His focus on creating a financial environment that builds on strong positive cash flow has saved not only LifeCare but also many other companies who have found themselves in a distressed cash flow situation.

His wisdom, troubleshooting, and mediation skills have been vital in finding amicable win-win solutions throughout the company, whether in a board meeting or dealing with contract issues. His most significant role in my life over the last eight years, however, has been career and life coach. Raye and I count Bill and his wife, Kathy, among our most cherished friendships.

Dan Finley
Board of Directors, Secretary, LifeCare Foundations
Heart and Compassion
Dan's compassion for the disadvantaged fuels his advocacy for those with learning challenges, handicap challenges, and those suffering from mental illness. He's a man with a tremendous heart who serves from a place of love.

Dan does not hesitate to go the extra mile to accommodate someone in need. We have known each other for over twenty-eight years now since that first meeting at Trinity Elementary. If you'll remember, Dan was one of the confirmations God sent my way in those early Nashville days and remains one of my dearest friends.

Jeff Parrish
Board of Directors, New Project Management,
LifeCare Foundations
Planner, Doer, Fixer

Prior to joining our board of directors, Jeff was my neighbor. As I got to know Jeff, I realized we needed his specific skill set working for LifeCare. He literally knows how to fix just about anything. Not only that, he understands the world of renovation, construction, and building codes. When LifeCare needs a renovation, a new home for seniors, or a facility for young people with rehabilitative needs, Jeff is right there, ensuring the safety, well-being, and comfort of our clients remains the priority during the entire project.

Jeff and his wife, Darlene, are treasured family friends. In fact, my parents have adopted them into the Mauck family.

One of the most unselfish and hardworking men I've had the privilege of knowing, Jeff works long hours with his own business yet is always available for LifeCare needs.

Bruce Boder
Board Member, LifeCare Foundations
Kingdom-Minded with a 40,000-Foot Perspective

Bruce has a passion for kingdom work. His "heart-and-head" approach to every decision involves both understanding God's purposes and thinking through every angle possible before moving forward.

Many times, Bruce has asked the important questions no one else has considered, and it's prompted a shift or change in the direction we were going. He doesn't just work toward solutions. His goal is the absolute best answer and has an uncanny ability to see the bigger picture.

Bruce's understanding of government, housing regulations, and legal issues have been essential to the growth of LifeCare. Bruce's friendship is invaluable to both Raye Ann and me.

Eddy Richey
Former Chairman of the Board of Directors, LifeCare Family Services
Wisdom, Discernment, and Business Sense

Although no longer an active board member, Eddy was a vital member during one of our most difficult seasons in the history of our company. His wisdom in charting a path through our most troubling circumstances helped our company remain intact.

Eddy was a huge encouragement and a trusted confidant to me personally in a potentially crushing time. His leadership and wisdom forged a plan that moved our company from being in jeopardy in 2009, to a safe harbor. I'm not sure where we would be today without Eddy's contributions to Lifecare during that time. So, if I never said it before, I'll say it now — from the bottom of my heart, thank you, Eddy.

Rebecca Foster
LifeCare Advisor
Advocate for Senior Care Services
Character and Integrity

Rebecca is exceptionally knowledgeable in the area of aging and issues of elderly care. Over the last ten years, Rebecca has kept me apprised of assessment, transition, and appropriate care issues for our seniors. She has tangible, firsthand experience in understanding and navigating these areas of the insurance and health care system, having been the primary caretaker for our Aunt Wanda and Aunt Marce. Even in the middle of difficult personal circumstances, my cousin has always been available with exceptional insight when I had a question regarding caring for the elderly.

Ernest Robertson
Treasurer, LifeCare and LifeCare Foundations
Encouragement and Dependability

I have been truly blessed by my in-laws, Ernie and Anne. It was Ernie who handled the build out of our first office in Smyrna in 1997, with the help of my father, Louie. Ernie also served on both LifeCare and LifeCare Foundation's boards for over twenty-two years. In fact, he was the first official board member for our companies. In those twenty-two years of service, he missed only one meeting, and that was due to an email server going down, preventing him from receiving the email about a date and time change. On my birthday, June 4, 2018, Ernie passed away, and I miss him every day.

Navigating Your Story

Every day I realize how blessed I am to live and walk through life with so many great people. Whether building a company or building your life, surrounding yourself with the right people is essential. Outside of family, these are the people you do life with, the people who know you, sometimes better than you know yourself, the people who aren't afraid to play devil's advocate, present the opposing side or push back.

When I joined the Eagles, I didn't get a group of "yes men" that all had the same opinions and beliefs. These men held varied views on government, business, and yes, even religion. In sharing and expressing differences of opinion, an air of respect and a desire to understand was always present.
So how do you find your own crew? The saying, "Birds of a feather flock together," comes to mind. First, you need be the kind of crew member you want to have.

AVAILABILITY

Time. Such a valuable commodity these days. We are pulled in every direction by family, by work, by church, by the world. Many things that demand our time and beckon for attention are good things, but are they all God things for us? That is the question.

To that end, I've learned that God is more interested in our availability than our abilities, accumulations, and accomplishments. While I've done my best to walk in wisdom, more importantly, I've just tried to make my time and efforts available to keep myself focused and dedicated to the calling and purpose, to opportunities that furthered that purpose, to the people who help carry them out, and those impacted by my purpose.

I didn't know any better than to give up. I just kept making myself available.

Are you available?

ACCOUNTABILITY

As the saying goes, so goes the truth. No man is an island. Men tend to be self-sufficient and self-contained. The power of wealth, lust, and love of money that men face is very real. It follows that it is of the utmost importance for you to have men who also face the same temptations, who hold you accountable and encourage you so that you don't succumb.

For me, this was the Eagles, not yes men. It's men who will check in with you, check under your hood, make sure you are running on all cylinders. I don't mean that as a sexist statement to the exclusion of women but one based on my own experience as a man.

Make no mistake, man or woman, the more you pursue Godly purpose and calling, the more the enemy pursues you. You need these people in your life.

Do you have accountability built into your life?

PASSION AND PURPOSE

What *are* the God things? Knowing the difference between good things and what a God thing is for you can save you from meaningless pursuits, wasted efforts, and lack of impact. It protects you from unnecessary overcommitment because purpose gives a lens to thoroughly evaluate every opportunity.

What energizes you? What stimulates your creativity? What excites you when you wake up in the morning? What do you find yourself wishing you were doing?

Conversely, what drains you? What sucks the life out of you? What makes you wish you were doing something else?

Knowing these things about yourself are crucial to keeping your decisions in line with your passion and purpose. If you've never defined a mission statement, I highly recommend you do so to define your passion and purpose further.

What are your passion and purpose?

FAITHFULNESS

Faithfulness is the cousin of availability. Faithfulness implies stability, dependability, and devotion to someone or something. Without faithfulness, being available can be a passing feeling, a whim, something that comes and goes. If your availability isn't secured faithfully to your passion and purpose, any task potentially becomes a burden. It gets less than our best.

When faithfulness is tied to your passion, to quote Winston Churchill, you will, "Never, never give up!"

Whether starting a business, developing a ministry, focusing on family, fatherhood, motherhood, or your marriage, faithfulness is the devotion and determination to walk with integrity and see it through to its full potential.

Are you faithful?

Charted Steps

1. First, think about the answers to the four questions above. Are you available? Do you have accountability in your life? What are your passion and purpose? Are you faithful to your passion and purpose? Write down your thoughts, pray over your answers, and ask the Lord for clarity.
2. Think about your crew. Write down the names of three to five individuals in your life who share your vision and purpose. These are people with whom you do life and can depend on. If you are already working toward a common goal, let them know how much you appreciate them personally and for their contributions. Do some dreaming together, and pray for guidance as you move forward.
3. Identify your Eagles. Name three to five people in your life who love you, will keep you accountable, provide guidance and support to you, and who you would give permission to speak into your life. If you aren't already in an accountability relationship with them, pray about approaching these people to put some structure and purpose around the relationship.

CHAPTER

10

The Admirals Club

"If I have seen further than others, it is by standing on the shoulders of giants."

— ISAAC NEWTON

"**Y**A KNOW, KENNY, THIS DIDN'T JUST HAPPEN."

With a potted shrub in hand, my friend Don stood next to me on the sidewalk in front of my new home in a beautiful, wooded subdivision in Franklin. He surveyed the results of his green thumb in action.

Viewing the landscape and wiping the sweat off my forehead with my sleeve, I shook my head in agreement. "No, no it didn't, Don. Thanks so much, I'd be lost without your help."

"I don't mean the yard," he chuckled, nodding toward the beautiful home in front of us as he knelt down to dig another hole for an azalea. I contemplated his response while watching him shovel the soft dirt. Then my gaze turned to the house.

Since I was a ten-year-old fifth grader in Flint, Michigan, Don Evans has been a mentor presence in my life, encouraging me to excel and challenging me to step outside my comfort zone. He and my dad taught me to play golf, but the lessons I learned about life and myself were far greater than any game of golf we ever played.

When I considered following in his footsteps and getting my master's degree, he said, "You can do this."

Don was instrumental in me landing my first teaching job. It was Don and his wife who helped Raye and me pack up when we moved from Flint to Nashville to answer a calling and fulfill a promise. Don was there when I had $750 and a dream and told me again, "You can do this."

Twenty-two years and a lot of water under the bridge later, here he was once again, an affirming influence in my life, encouraging me, stretching me, and lending hands of support.

I looked down at my friend doing what he does best, serving those he loves, and smiled. I might have even fought off a few tears.

"No, this didn't just happen, did it, Don?"

Influencers

Influencers come into our lives and change our trajectory. Influencers show us the possibilities, lead us to the edge of ourselves, and inspire us to become more. Influencers challenge us not to be content with the status quo. They motivate us to forge into new territory, to create a legacy like no other for those who come behind us just as they have done before us.

I've had many influencers in my life, a few of whom are listed in this chapter. Some, like Don, entered my life naturally through regular, everyday circumstances. I was a student; he was a teacher. I intentionally sought out others for a specific purpose or advice, and in the end, gained a mentor and friend, as I did with Dr. Tim Clinton.

Dr. Tim Clinton
American Association of Christian Counselors, President
James Dobson Family Institute, Executive Director

Making a difference in the lives of others was my primary goal as Director of Counseling at Christ Church in 1996. I set out on a quest to connect with as many like-minded ministries and people as I could. I wanted to learn everything possible from those who had already built counseling networks and were already making a difference in other cities, states, and even on the national level.

I scoured not only my home state of Tennessee but also national databases for people and organizations that fit the bill. After compiling my list, I decided to start with a national organization in Virginia, to glean what I could from their incorporation of counseling and care with their national ministry. Unfortunately, I didn't find what I was looking for and went back to my hotel a little discouraged.

Then the Lord brought to mind a name I had heard at a recent seminar, Tim Clinton. Then I remembered he was also in Virginia. Tim was Vice President of the American Association of Christian Counselors (AACC).

What the heck, what have I got to lose? I thought. *The worst that can happen is he won't return my call.*

Tim graciously took my call. Even better, he invited me to tour his own counseling practice and suggested we go to lunch after the tour. That's when I learned Tim was a visionary.

He talked about his role as a leader of the Liberty University Counseling Program and listened as I shared about my fledgling company and dreams. More importantly, through the course of our conversation, Tim opened my eyes to the opportunities and the national potential for faith-based mental health professionals and organizations.

Turns out, Tim Clinton was the real reason I was supposed to go to Virginia. I learned something else that trip. Chutzpah. Sometimes, you just have to make the big ask...or the big call. If there is someone you know you can learn from, that you know will help you carry out your calling and God-given dream, in humility, get yourself in front of them. Learn from them.

What if I chickened out and hadn't made that call, excused it away or even let my disappointment at my original reason for traveling to Virginia shut me down? I would have missed out on not just a great learning opportunity, but an amazing mentorship and a lifelong friendship.

Tim is now President of the American Association of Christian Counselors. Under his visionary leadership, the AACC is now the largest and fastest growing international Christian counseling network and conference organization in the world. Over twenty-two years of our friendship, I've had a front-row seat to the unfolding of his vision for his practice and the mental health care landscape in America and globally. Tim's an inspiration to watch, and his mentorship has been an indispensable asset as I have navigated the growth of my own health care company.

Tim and I have had similar experiences in our walk with God. Both of us realized the need to free ourselves from someone riding on the coattails of someone else's faith to encounter God personally. Tim's dad was highly influential in that process for him:

My greatest influencer would have to be my father, Reverend James Clinton. My dad was a larger-than-life man and an integral part of my understanding of faith and God. One of the greatest gifts Dad ever gave me was his emphasis on keeping God and family first in life. This is our Clinton family heritage.

When Dad became ill, I fell into a season of questioning. Why was God taking Dad now? How would I stand in my faith without him to hold me up? I shared my doubts and questions with my dad. I told him this was too hard, and I couldn't imagine my life without him in it. Dad encouraged me, telling me that my understanding would grow over time. Honestly, I wasn't exactly sure about that answer.

After Dad's passing, I went away to a favorite retreat, an old family cabin in the mountains of Pennsylvania. I needed time and space to process and come to grips with losing such an important part of my life. I questioned God about a lot of things and actually left a little disappointed because I felt I hadn't heard back.

But as I was coming down the mountain headed home, God spoke to my heart with this question: "Will I be the God of your father to you or be the God of you and your father?"

Breakthrough. In that moment, I released my heart fully and completely, a gift I'm sure Dad was smiling about from heaven.

Ken Abraham
Eighteen-Time New York Times Best-Selling Author
National Speaker

Ken was an Eagle and remains an "iron sharpens iron" friend. Through the years, we've encouraged each other as fathers, husbands, and Christian men walking out our faith in professions that constantly challenged our Christian worldview.

I've watched Ken and his wife, Lisa, actively live their faith day in and day out for over twenty-three years and how they have poured into family, those they lead at church, and into their community.

Writing this book has stretched me every way possible, and my friend Ken's expertise and advice as a best-selling author have been extremely helpful on this journey. For a guy who is one of the most prolific writers, with publishers, well-known celebrities and leaders clamoring for him to write their next book, Ken is one of the most unassuming, humble people I know.

A man of integrity, he carefully chooses his work, never compromising his beliefs just to take on a writing project or endorse a book when asked.

You'll never hear Ken drop a name in a conversation. So, I'll do it for him. Ken's best-seller list includes: *Let's Roll!* with Lisa Beamer; *No Dream Is Too High* with Astronaut Buzz Aldrin; *Your Best Life Now* by Joel Olsteen; *Between Heaven and the Real World* with Steven Curtis Chapman; *Against All Odds* with Chuck Norris; *True Faith and Allegiance* by Attorney General Roberto Gonzalez; and a wonderful book titled *When Your Parent Becomes Your Child* chronicling with humor and care, Ken's own experiences and challenges in caring for his mother who suffered from Alzheimer's disease.

One of Ken's legacy influencers comes from his college days:

"Dr. Dennis Kinlaw, President of Asbury College, has been one of the most influential people in my life. Dr. Kinlaw's life itself was an example to me of what a Christian man should be. His ability to articulate his knowledge of God's Word encouraged me in my biblical studies at Asbury and encouraged me to be the best writer I could be."

Don Marsh
University of South Florida, Assistant Track Coach

One of the most enthusiastic, encouraging men and influencers of my life is my Kearsley High School Track Coach, Mr. Don Marsh. Coach Marsh personally invested himself in his athletes, coming out on the track, arms pumping in the air, whooping it up, and clapping as we arrived. He stretched out with us, jogged around the track with us (still clapping his hands enthusiastically), and gave us the proverbial slap on the back while exclaiming, "It's a great day!"

Coach Marsh ran right alongside us, striking up a conversation, asking how our day was, how we were doing, and spurring us on to a great practice. Coach was always prepared with a plan for each of us that was specific to our event. Even in a highly individualized sport, Coach Marsh always stressed the impact of our individual performance on the team as a whole.

Coach saw something in me even when I couldn't see it myself. I was a hard worker but didn't have a lot of confidence in myself as a runner. He pushed me beyond what I thought possible. It paid off. I set the school record my senior year in the 330 low hurdles and placed second at the Big Nine Regional Championship.

Looking back, I can see how Coach wasn't just invested in me as an athlete; he poured himself into me as a young man off the track. He encouraged me to excel academically and found qualities in each and every one of his athletes outside of track to applaud.

Coach attended my graduation party, came to my wedding, and bought gifts for both. I'm quite sure I'm not the only one.

Coach's investment in me continued paying dividends in my life. When things got tough at Mott Community College, the University of Michigan, or while pursuing my masters, I heard Coach Marsh telling me to run like the wind, that hurdle was just another obstacle to fly over. When I felt like giving up during that horrible season of losing everything, when I had eleven government attorneys trying to recoup over a million dollars for our company, the qualities of perseverance and endurance he reinforced in me kicked in and carried me through.

Don is in his twenty-first year as an assistant coach at the University of South Florida, specializing in the pole vault and long jump. He has coached seven All-Americans, fourteen national qualifiers, sixteen conference qualifiers, sixteen conference champions, and forty-four regional qualifiers. Before USF, Don coached three years at Saginaw Valley State University, where he had four All Americans in the high jump, pole vault, and 400 meters. Before Saginaw, Don coached at Flint Kearsley High School for twenty-five years, building one of the premier track-and-field programs in the state of Michigan. He's Michigan's Track Coach of the Year for 1974, 1978, and 1992, in addition to the entire Midwest Track Coach of the Year in 1992. He was also a finalist National High School Track Coach of the Year in 1992, and has been inducted into Michigan's Track Coaches Hall of Fame with multiple honors.

I asked Coach Marsh who he considered the top influencer in his life, and he wrote back with two:

"Without a doubt, my dad is at the top of the list. A quiet, principled man, I learned self-discipline through his example. Dad attended all my high school and college meets when he could, always the encourager but never trying to motivate me by pushing too hard.

My dad was one of the most intelligent men I knew and could do things I couldn't with a master's degree. The fact that Dad came from humble beginnings and only had an eighth-grade education only makes me love and respect him more for who he was and what he did for his family. I miss my Dad every day!

Number two on my list is my own high school coach, Mac Gobel, the legendary football and track coach from my high school in Charlotte, Michigan. When I went out for track in ninth grade, I was scared because of his reputation of being a tough disciplinarian. But we became close, and he helped me prepare to win the state championship in the quarter mile and encouraged me to run at Michigan State University. He is also the one who suggested I teach and coach, which led me to fifty-eight years of coaching track. I still think of him and the life lessons he taught me to this day!"

Eric Strickland
3 LS, President and CEO

In the fall of 2013, I began to think about the long-term interests of LifeCare Family Services employees and staff. Our company was doing great in terms of contracts and net revenue; however, I needed an exit strategy that provided an excellent retirement program for all our employees, not just the executives of the company who could afford an independent retirement plan.

An associate introduced me to Eric Strickland, thinking Eric's innovative strategies for retirement for his own company might be something that might work for LifeCare. On a beautiful fall day, I met with the young CEO and President of Omni Visions. I told Eric I was looking for a good retirement program for my employees and had been told he had some creative solutions.

Eric, in turn, explained that his company was an employee-owned company, offering each employee ownership in the form of stocks. Those who remained faithful for the long term were receiving significant payouts at retirement. I spoke with some of the employees planning to retire who confirmed that the plan was indeed working well.

I didn't know when I first contacted Eric, but found out that day, that Omni was looking to partner with a company like ours. Turns out, our companies were a perfect fit. On October 1, 2014, Eric and I shook hands as LifeCare and Omni became one of the largest growing child and family programs in Tennessee and the

Southeast region. Currently, we are looking at working together to expand nationwide over the next decade.

I am ten years Eric's senior; nonetheless, he is one of the wisest men I know not only in business, but also as a leader. Eric knows how to empower those he leads. I am thankful God has chosen to bring us together as partners.

What began as seeking advice ended in finding not only precisely what I was looking for — a long-term solution for our employees — but also a long-term solution for the company, one that allows our legacy company to land safely under Eric's wise and visionary leadership. Eric will take our company to heights in providing excellent care for millions of children and families.

When asked who the most influential person in his life has been, here's what Eric had to say:

"The most impactful person in my life is my father, Louis "Butch" Strickland, a humble migrant farm worker from Northwest Georgia, with a servant's heart. Butch wanted to study accounting but chose to work to take care of us, his family. His faithful commitment to family and his willingness to work long, hard hours characterize the great man my dad was.

My father also coached me in baseball and basketball and served as a scoutmaster, guiding many young men to Eagle Scout honors. He earned the highest adult scouting honor as a "Silver Beaver," all while working more than full-time at a ten-to-twelve-dollar-an-hour job.

I'll always remember my dad for his strong character. He proved to me every day of his life that no matter where you are by the world's standards, you can make a huge difference in the life of others!"

Mark White
Representative, Tennessee State House of Representatives

"May I call you Dad?" These five words written on a post-it note embody a lifetime of work for my friend Mark White.

I have known Mark White since he was elected to the Tennessee House of Representatives in 2010. As a representative for the Memphis area, Mark channels his passion for at-risk children into authored bills and amendments supporting our most vulnerable children in foster care, health, and behavioral health care services. In an area that trends Democratic, a Republican and a man of Godly character has earned the trust of his constituents and their vote by representing the district well. Mark is deeply respected on both sides of the aisle.

His passion for at-risk children took an unexpected turn on a mission trip with his church to Panama. Poverty created a cycle of teen pregnancy, children without father figures to look up to, and youth becoming enslaved in trafficking. Very few opportunities for education existed. Moved by the extended effects of poverty on Panamanian children and families, Mark immediately began laying the groundwork for a nonprofit to provide future educational opportunities with the goal of helping families break the cycle of poverty. Today, his nonprofit ensures children the opportunity for elementary, middle, and high school, and even college.

Mark and his family have had the privilege of hosting children assisted by his nonprofit. One such child came to Tennessee for a college visit with her mother and spent a few days with the White family. Shortly after her departure, Mark found an envelope addressed to him. Unfolding the letter inside, a bright pink sticky note at the bottom caught his attention. It read, "May I call you Dad?" For hundreds of children in Panama, this is the real impact of Mark's work.

Mark's main influencer in his life:

"While there are many people in each of our lives we could mention that *influence us to be the kind of person we become, I will highlight my father, Hoyt White, as my main influencer. When I was five years old, my father moved our family from Union City, Tennessee, to Nashville to attend David Lipscomb College and never turned back from ministry or from his dedication to preaching the Gospel.*

Growing up observing his faith, seeing it lived out as he led our family, taught me the importance of a strong Christ-centered father in the home. His example inspired my book May I Call You Dad: Why Fathers Are Needed in the Home. *Having worked with children as a teacher, principal, and in mission work, I have learned that the absence of a father, especially a Christ-centered father, leaves a child lacking in their ability to meet the responsibilities and challenges of life. I learned from my father that we must be engaged in all areas: the home, the church, community, and politics. Most social ills that face our communities today could be addressed by a responsible, God-fearing father in the home."*

One Thing in Common

Each of these people is an admiral in my book. From entry-level positions, each has worked their way up the ranks, plotted a course, built a powerful team, weathered the storms and conquered, so to speak. Each one of them has powerfully shaped my personal life and affected the course of LifeCare. Some I can say, "I knew them when..." Others were already at the top of their game when the Lord directed me to their door at just the right time, when I needed guidance and even education in a specific area.

In each of these men's stories, one thing stands out to me. Did you notice? One common thread the majority share was an influential father figure. When asked about influencers in their own lives, the majority included Dad in the list. While having a strong parental figure is indeed not a prerequisite for success, it does emphasize the importance of the role many of us hold in our own children's lives while they are with us and then continuing on once they embark on their own voyage.

My own list of top influencers would be incomplete without adding some of my individual family members, including my father and father-in-law. Not every man can count his father-in-law among the positive influencers in his life. I am fortunate to be one who can.

Ernest Robertson
My Father-In-Law

"Ern," I said, choosing my words carefully, "I know you might not want to talk about it, but I want to ask you about your time in the service and your tour in Vietnam. I don't want to push, but if you would, it would be an honor to hear your story."

Ernie stared off into the distance for a moment and then thoughtfully began.

"Well, there was one time we were setting up for camp along a river, and we saw the Viet Cong on the other side setting up mortars and larger guns. We thought it might be a rough night because through our high-powered binoculars, it looked like the guns might be pointed in our position. We figured if we're watching them, they're watchin' us. So, we found a little bunker that was hidden behind some trees that we thought was out of the sight of any scouts. But only six men could fit comfortably, and there were fifteen of us that needed shelter. So, we told the men to go back and just act normal, like they were settling in for the night to sleep, but once night fell, to quickly and quietly fall back about a hundred yards to the bunker.

"Just as soon as night fell, sure enough, the shelling and rounds were coming in from everywhere. Machine gunshots zipping and bombs exploding, grenade launchers, and all kinds of firepower came in all around us. But all fifteen of us were safely crammed eye to eye in that bunker, not making a sound. The shooting finally stopped in the wee hours of the morning while it was still dark, and we snuck out of there as fast as we could."

My father-in-law Ernie died on June 4, 2018, while I was in the middle of writing this book. Ernie served on both boards (Life-Care Foundations and LifeCare Family Services) for over twenty-two years. In fact, Ernie was the first board member selected.

It was Ernie and my own father, Louie, who built out our garage as our first office in Smyrna, Tennessee, in 1997. That was just like him, using his skills as a carpenter to serve and love his family. Ernie built a treehouse for the kids and a deck with a screened-in porch. When we opened up "real" offices, he was there, building out rooms, putting together tables, computer desks, and filing cabinets.

Ernie loved spending time with his son, fishing and hunting. He hid little miniature cars in his pockets for the grandkids to find and loved to beat me in the card game Euchre. His wife of forty-two years, Ann, his daughter Raye, and his son Brent and their families were his life.

Action movies were also a love of Ernie's. That's why, about a month or so before his passing, I had called him and suggested we spend the day together watching a few of his favorites. As we headed to the kitchen to replenish our snacks and drinks after the first movie, I decided to ask Ernie about something we'd never really talked about before, and he shared that story.

Ernie sat there when he was done talking, lost in his thoughts for a moment. I broke in and said, "You keep saying, 'We,' but I believe it was you who saved those men that night."

He turned his head with an uncomfortable smile. That was the way of my father-in-law, not wanting to take credit.

Up until his death, I had thought Ernie had one bronze star. I now know he actually was awarded four bronze stars. I think I know where he earned one of them.

Brad and Candy Rainwater
My Sister and Brother-in-Law

Brad and Candy have huge hearts and an exceptional ability and capacity to love unconditionally. For years, they have done just that.

Brad's coach position offers plenty of opportunities to love on student athletes. Some of these athletes have been given a clinical label of a learning or social disability, yet they have managed to overcome the stigma of that diagnosis and excelled in sports and in life. Coach Rainwater and his wife have many times been more of an adopted mom and dad or aunt and uncle to the kids that come into their lives.

Their love is not just centered on helping other children. It starts in their own home. Their grandson, Bradley, is legally blind. With Brad and Candy cheering him on and being present with hands-on assistance, Bradley has learned to ride a bike, is an excellent student, and even does the pole vault. Not only that, he is an outstanding piano player.

Brad and Candy took me in as a young university student. It's a way of life for them — providing a safe place, a meal, or a bed for someone in need. I watched as my sister and her husband put love into action by doing and being there for so many like myself, and it inspired me. It continues to inspire me.

Brad and Candy provide not only a safe harbor but a lighthouse — a beacon of hope — to so many.

"Big Lou" and Melonee Mauck
My Parents

Without question, my parents have been the most influential of anyone in my life. Every day, I carry with me the love, support, commitment, and encouragement I experienced as a child.

Mom was a living example to me of true "unconditional love." She prayed with me at bedtime and over me while I was sleeping, fixed my favorite foods, pretended to feed my imaginary friend, and made sure I always had clean clothes for school and church and a clean uniform for all my sports practices and games.

When I was sick, Mom fixed me her famous potato soup, her favorite healing recipe. I aced writing papers all throughout school, mainly because Mom applied her editing skills and attention to detail before I turned anything in, helping me correct what I had missed.

More importantly, it was watching the way Mom lived her life and sowed into others that influenced me most. I heard my mom spend untold hours on phone calls while I played on the kitchen floor. She wasn't talking as much as she was listening to friends and family pour out troubles and hurts. Mom gave her friends encouraging words of comfort, affirmation, and prayers. She was there for them. Although a sermon from my pastor and a promise to an inner-city child pushed me to start a faith-based agency, my mom's continual encouragement prompted me to actually walk out the door and close out that $650 savings account.

All those caught listening skills, built by watching my mom just be who she was growing up, are now a part of my DNA. I don't believe I would have been a therapist if not for the influence of my mother's example.

"Your mom may one day kick me out of the bedroom, but she'll never kick me out of our home. That, I can promise you." I've lost count of how many times my dad said that to us when we were kids, many times after my parents argued in front of us.

The pain of his own story gave my father perspective and purpose in his own life and only strengthened his commitment to his own family. Growing up abandoned by his own father and lacking the paternal affirmations we are wired to receive fueled my father's determination not to repeat the same pattern. Unlike his father before him, he has kept that promise for over sixty-three years. That kind of commitment left an indelible mark on our family.

When Dad moved to Nashville from Michigan after retiring, I approached him with the idea of assisting with the building and grounds needs of LifeCare. The company had started purchasing buildings instead of leasing space, and the demand for someone to oversee the facilities was growing. The ex-CEO in Dad rose to the occasion, accepting and accomplishing every task asked of him, and has continued to do so for over eighteen years.

Dad has made his mark on not only the company but also the people of LifeCare during those years. His commitment, encouragement, and sense of humor have earned him the nickname "Big Lou."

Navigating Your Story

Each influencer listed has spoken into my life at a critical juncture, at a time when I needed to know more, do more, be more than I was in that moment. I wish I could say that every time I found myself in that place, I was prepared to hear what I needed to hear and see what I needed to see.

Three words come to mind when I think about those times. I've been completely open when I've heard and seen beyond myself and moved forward in significant ways.

MOTIVATION

Both external and internal forces motivate us to pursue knowledge and change. They were do or die, sink or swim, stay where I was and be safe, or step out in faith and take the risk to go to the next level. These were times when I found myself highly motivated, and the Lord brought just the right person into my life, the person with the skills and knowledge I needed to learn to take the work He had given me further than I ever could have on my own.

When we lost our largest client and were sitting on seven digits of accounts receivables owed? I was literally faced with layoffs, major cutbacks, and potentially closing the doors. This was the season I gave the used book to Dave Ramsey. My motivation to survive was extremely high. That's when Mark White came into my life, helping us navigate the legal system...and I learned.

When I realized the vision the Lord had for Lifecare far surpassed my own? I had a choice to settle for where we were or pay attention and be obedient to the calling on my life. The promise I made to Carlos continued to be my motivation to move forward instead of settling. It drove me to learn everything I could about the national platform for mental health care and led me to Virginia. It was the Lord who led me to Tim Clinton while there...and I learned.

What is your current motivation?

TEACHABILITY

All the right information can be swirling around you; all the right people can be in proximity; everything you need to succeed at whatever it is God has called you to might be right there at your fingertips. But it's worthless if you don't have a teachable heart.

Being teachable is a foundational part of growth — in character development, personally, and in business. Without the quality and heart position of being teachable, it doesn't matter who comes across your path; you won't hear or accept what they have to offer.

Listening is a skill so lacking in today's today's culture, but it is an essential quality an essential quality in a teachable person. A good listener *is not distracted and is present in the moment.* Are you focused on what the other person is saying or on what you are having for lunch, what you are going to say next or your to-do list for the rest of the day? Are you constantly checking your phone, or do you put your phone on *Do Not Disturb* during meetings and conversations with others? Better yet, do you leave it out of sight altogether? Are you continually paying more attention to what's going on around you and who is walking by than the person in front of you?

A good listener does not interrupt, finish others' sentences, or derail the conversation. It follows that if you're actively listening, you'll have questions, and you'll respond to what's being said authentically, both verbally and through body language but not at the expense of finishing the other party's sentences.

Are you teachable?

HUMILITY

Above all else, humility. Humility goes hand in hand with being teachable and a good listener. It's a biblical mandate for the believer stated in 1 Peter 5:5b, "... Clothe yourselves, all of you, with humility toward one another, ..." (ESV).

Humility knows, well, that it does not know it all. You can't think you know it all and be teachable. Humility considers the needs of others. One can't always be thinking of themselves in a conversation and truly be listening. Exercising humility implies action. It implies self-restraint. It implies intention.

Humility also recognizes the grace, the gifts, the forgiveness, and the favor that has been bestowed along the way. It considers itself not more worthy than the next person to receive any of it. Now that I own my own business, I find people come to me from time to time as I have gone to my influencers. More than ever, the above principles still apply.

Do you exercise humility?

Charted Steps

IMPRINT: Influencers and Mentors

This chapter and the previous have similarities. Both are about finding *your* people as you carry out your life purpose and mission. Remember these?

Rule number one: Don't just find people. Find **your** *people.*
Rule number two: Find your Eagles.

Now add:

Rule number three: Find your influencers.

Let's explore who the influencers are in your own life.

1. First, think about the answers to these questions:

    - Are you motivated to learn?
    - Are you teachable? Why or why not?
    - Do you exercise humility?

    Write your thoughts down, pray over your answers, and ask the Lord for help. Be completely honest about where you are in this.

2. List five people who come to mind who have been a major influence in your life.

3. Write a paragraph or two under each name, briefly telling each story.

4. Be intentional. Make a plan to reach out to each person on your list, and thank them for what they have meant to you. Ask if they would be willing to share about the person who has had the greatest impact on their own life.

CHAPTER

11

Captain's Log

"Letters are among the most significant memorial a person can leave behind them."

— JOHANN WOLFGANG VON GOETHE

"DADDY, YOU WANT TO HEAR my scripture verse I learned today? It's not too hard." My KelseyGirl, in all her bouncy curls and bubbly personality, sat in the back seat looking at me in the rearview mirror.

"Well, sure, honey. What is it?" I waited in anticipation of some cute misquoted paraphrase.

"Psalms 139:14. We are awesome and wonderfully made," she stated clearly and concisely with the cutest childlike confidence.

Walking the wooded paths around the pond behind our home this fall afternoon, I'm remembering that car ride. I had picked up Kelsey from church after Vacation Bible School that afternoon. I remember buckling her in as she sat there examining her hands. After she shared that verse, we talked about the uniqueness of each person God created, the fact that no two fingerprints are alike.

Taking a seat on a nearby log, feeling the breeze pass, hearing the bending of the reeds, and breathing in the clean air, I am reminded just how fast my life and that of my family is passing by right in front of me. My oldest daughter, Megan, now has three children of her own. Landon, my son, constantly travels following the demands of his job, and my youngest daughter, Kelsey, is finding her place in this world as an adult.

All these thoughts swirl around my head as I look down at my own hands. Then it hits me — DNA. God makes each of us with unique DNA, just as our stories carry unique DNA. Our stories carry both a strand from our past and a strand from our present.

One person's story DNA is a distinct imprint like no one else. We all carry not only unique physical DNA, we carry just as unique story DNA that in God's hands, is being shaped into something miraculous and beautiful, even if we can't see it yet. So, yes, my sweet Kelsey girl, we truly are all awesome and wonderfully made.

A New Tradition

A few years ago at Christmas, I unknowingly initiated a new tradition in my family. I had been searching for a way to make sure my children knew exactly what they meant to Raye and me. As much as I am capable, I wanted to let them know their God-given uniqueness, their awesome-and-wonderfully-made-ness, exactly what we saw in each of them that made them special in the world and significant in our eyes, to have something they could turn to, hold in their hands, and reflect on when life told them otherwise, a tangible encouragement that would last beyond our lifetime as parents. I wrote them each a letter.

Christmas Eve, I gathered the family around and had each one open their letter, and we read them as a family. Imagine one of those warm and fuzzy Hallmark movie moments, family gathered by a cozy fire, grandchildren scattered at the feet of the patriarch of the family, everyone smiling with misty eyes as each letter is read by Grandpa.

This was not that.

It was the awkward, uncomfortable, no one wanting to make eye contact, kids asking to use the restroom, everyone squirming in their seat moment from a Christmas comedy. Vulnerability can be like that at first, but fast-forward through several Christmas Eves, and now it's a family time looked forward to and cherished.

Those first letters were as hard to write as they were for my family to sit through. I filled the wastebasket to overflowing with failed attempts. Once I quit trying to find the right words, though, or the words I thought my children would want me to say, and dug down deep into the memories we've made together and spoke from my heart, the words flowed easily.

Landon Kent Mauck
April 17, 1985 –

Landon is my firstborn and my one and only son. When Landon was born, I'm pretty sure Hans and the rest of my great-grandfathers were high fiving and throwing a party up in heaven – the Mauck name would live on. Well, I imagine they would have, but in all seriousness, carrying on the family name was extremely important to me, and Landon was a fulfillment of that desire.

Landon's entry into this world was not an easy one. Weighing in at nine pounds, eleven ounces, he was a big baby, and Raye Ann is a little woman. After hours of labor with little progress, the doctors determined she would need a cesarean delivery and fast.

Honestly, I was not prepared for what happened next. I remember standing by her side, holding her hand, watching the doctors begin to perform the operation. As the doctor wielded the knife and begin making the incision, I began feeling a little dizzy. I must have turned white as a sheet because the nurse took one look at me and said, "Honey, you might want to sit down."

Working quickly, the doctor soon reached inside Raye Ann and exclaimed, "Wow! I think this kid has a helmet on!"

Pulling and pushing in a manner that did not seem natural (or physically possible), the doctor attempted to get Landon turned around and out of Raye Ann.

Our usually jovial doctor was now no longer smiling. The atmosphere intensified as he asked for the forceps and continued pulling, pushing, and maneuvering what seemed like the entirety of both his arms inside my wife's abdomen. Finally after a few very intense and scary minutes, the doctor, sweating now from the workout, let out a huge sigh of relief and said, "I think he's finally turned upright."

Seconds later, out popped our beautiful, wonderfully handsome baby boy. (No biased parent here.) Immediately, Landon let the whole world know he was not happy to be removed from such a dark, warm, and secure place, plopped into this cold, bright place, and then get poked, prodded, measured, and wiped down.

When the nurse asked if I wanted to hold my son, I chuckled to myself. I don't know why they ask a father who's been waiting hundreds of days and spending considerable time and money buying the baby bed, baby rocker, stroller, diapers, and every other little thing needed, the question of if they want to hold their baby. Seems like a no brainer to me. Yet at the same time, I was speechless as I apprehensively held out my hands in a nonverbal cue. Landon didn't seem all too happy to see me as I embraced him, laughing and crying.

I was able to hold Landon only briefly before the nurses took him to check his bilirubin count and run through another gamit of newborn tests and checks. Instinctively falling back on my track days, I burst through the swinging double doors and down the hall at a full sprint. I didn't even stop to take off my scrubs.

I raced to the waiting room, excitedly announcing to friends, family, and anyone else in my path, *"We have a baby boy!"* As everyone hugged and celebrated, it really began to sink in. I was a dad for the first time, and it was a boy.

Raye Ann and I had made a deal. She named the girls, so I had the honor of naming our son. The name was picked out months prior. Our favorite show at the time was *Little House on the Prairie*, and Landon would be named after the actor who portrayed one of our favorite roles, Michael Landon.

Living life with Landon has been a joy. To my great delight, we share a love of sports, which has been the catalyst for many great memories. At first, he loved two things, his pacifier and playing with a ball. We started with a soft cushy baseball and bat, which he mostly chewed.

In the toddler years, we moved on to a preschool-sized slam-dunk basketball hoop and wrestling once I got home from work each night. When Landon turned five, the fun really began. I would take him to the elementary school across the street from our house, and we'd play for hours on the playground.

In his teen years, Landon developed a love of basketball. We would play often from daylight to dusk. He had a great shot, scoring often from outside and inside the paint, and was one of the most unselfish players on his team, always looking for the open man.

Over the years, Landon has learned to be a true team player in life, and to this day, his competitive and kind spirit have served him well. He has expertly transferred those life skills learned from competitive team sports to the corporate world, improving the quality of the work environment.

As a human resources administrator, and more recently as management at a senior-care facility, he searches for creative ways to include the entire team's ideas and input whenever possible. Landon has so much to offer, and one of the greatest values he has spoken into my life is his extreme faithfulness to family and friends.

> Dear Landon,
>
> One of the greatest joys in my life is being your father. I have so many great and wonderful memories made spending time with you. Holding you in my arms that first time, I never realized how fast my life and yours would fly by. It's hard to believe it's been over thirty years. From hearing your belly-laughing giggle while your sister tried unsuccessfully to tumble or roll over, to countless high-fives and games of H-O-R-S-E to admiring your great shooting ability as we played Aaround the World, I've treasured it all. Every moment you chose to hang with Dad as a little boy is a cherished memory, such as following me around every time I cut the grass, pretending to do the same with your toy mower as a four-year-old.
>
> When winter brought piles and piles of Michigan snow, you were right there with me with your little shovel, working up a sweat keeping up with dad. Watching the video of you riding your bike without the training wheels for the first time, me running beside you until you trusted me to let go, brings me the greatest joy.

Even when you fell, you got right back up. You never give up, a trait I know you will pass on to your own children.

An athlete myself, I was happy you loved sports. The times you and I went swimming, played one on-one basketball games until it was dark, and your mom called us in for dinner, all priceless memories. Now we enjoy golfing and watching a great college football game. The best part is not the game but simply throwing the football at halftime.

I never thought I was getting a little older until I put on my good running shoes and caught some of those passes like Odell Beckham! Remember a few years ago while watching the bowl games, you said, "Dad, something I've always wanted to do is go to the Rose Bowl. Can we go?"

Somehow, we were able to convince your mother this wasn't a crazy idea and even to go with us. Just like that, we were on our way to see Michigan play USC within a week at the Los Angeles Memorial Coliseum. I didn't even care that Michigan lost. I'll never forget that moment or that trip.

When your mom and I watched you in the ceremony after earning you MBA from Indiana Wesleyan, I was so proud. I am amazed at what you have accomplished so early in your life. Don't ever compare or let others compare you to me or anyone for that matter. God has a special calling specifically for your life, a wonderful journey meant just for you and your family. I hope you have great memories of you and I working together with LifeCare, and your great work as our human resources director. Landon, I gave you the most simplistic and menial entry-level job to start, and you soared with it. As I watched you pass on better paying offers and move on to your current position as a Human Resources Administrator for Lifecare, I was so proud. LifeCare wasn't able to compete with those salaries, but you stayed and remained faithful to our legacy company for fourteen years, helping build our staff to serve thousands upon thousands of children, couples, and families from all walks of life.

But what makes you stand out, other than your six-foot-four-inch height and great looks, obviously from your mom's side of the family, is your heart. You generously and quietly give to others financially or otherwise, never seeking public acknowledgement. I know you do these things as unto God, not anyone else. But I do see it, and I know more importantly, God sees your heart, and that's what makes you so special to us as your family.

By the way, I am so thankful that you have finally met the love of your life in Brittany. Your mom and I don't want to put any pressure on either of you, but to keep the Mauck legacy going, we are hoping for at least five grandchildren over the next five years. LOL

Landon, you're the best son a dad could hope for. I'm blessed and honored to be a father to a son that has exceeded way beyond all my expectations – thank you! I love you, Landon. Dream deep. Enjoy each moment of the sunrise, every soft breeze in the afternoon, and sunsets with a family as great as you three have been to your mother and me.

Thanks for being such a great part of our legacy story, Son!

Love, Dad

Megan De Ann Mauck-Hinson
July 7, 1987 –

I nicknamed our first daughter, Megan, "Sunshine," because she brought exactly that to the family each day. Megan was always full of surprises. Her middle name is a combination of my mother's middle name, Delois, and Raye Ann's mom's first name, Ann. As a baby, Megan was always ahead of the curve. Whether talking, walking, or reading, Megan did it sooner than the others.

She was an active child, always on the go, the one who got into every single unlocked closet, opened (and emptied) every drawer she could reach, and tried to climb out every window. At the age of two, it was not uncommon for our little busybody to make it all the way to the neighbor's house and knock on the door before we even realized she was gone. That's the way she rolled. We were that family that had to install all the extra special safety latches on our cabinets and baby gates on our steps.

Hand in hand with that activity was a stubborn streak. I'll never forget the day I realized we were in it for the long haul on that front. On this particular day, Megan kept pulling her brother's hair while he was sleeping. I had already asked her twice to stop pulling his hair. She did not stop, and eventually her pulling woke him up and made him cry. I looked her square in the eye and shook my finger as I said, "If you don't stop, I'm going to spank you," to which she turned her backside to me and bent over. I swatted her once on her pampered bottom.

Megan straightened up, looked at me, and proceeded to turn, and bent over again, as if to say, "Is that all you got?"

I was completely taken aback, and I tried so hard to keep a straight face and follow through. But I burst out laughing instead. Right then, I knew she was going to be my challenging one. On a side note, somehow, we got all of that on video!

Because of her bouncy curls, Megan has always reminded me of Shirley Temple. Megan liked to sing, too. We bought her a little karaoke machine, and Megan and her sister presented many a performance to the family. She also loved dancing. Raye Ann would help with her routines, and Megan won first place several times at her school talent shows.

Her love of performance stayed with her throughout her childhood and into high school. More times than I can count, I would be watching her singing and dancing her way through the house, and she would ask me to video her, to dance with her, to sing with her. She was an actress, a dancer, a singer, a reporter, a teacher... whatever it was, she was in charge.

In high school, Megan was the flier for her cheer squad. Don't ever let anyone tell you cheer isn't a sport. Wait until your daughter is tossed twenty feet in the air, plummeting back down with only the arms of a few high schoolers to break her fall. I think Raye Ann and I aged ten years in those four years, but she wouldn't have wanted any other position.

In addition to being the most active of our three children, Megan is without a doubt the most driven. All of that determination, tenacity, and spark have served her well in whatever she has chosen to pursue. For nine years, she has easily juggled being a teacher with a side home business. Her teaching, coupled with her natural performance ability, have opened the door for many opportunities, including a national commercial for ABCMouse.com.

On top of her multifaceted careers, Megan is a wonderful mother of three — our wonderful twin grandsons, Easton and Cooper, and our granddaughter, Gracelyn Hope. When I think of Gracelyn, I just have to smile. God has such a great sense of humor. Gracelyn is giving it back to Megan in heaping spoonfuls over what she gave to us.

> Megan,
>
> *I love you dearly. Your joyful energy from the time you were little has been such a delight to experience. The great joy you bring to your family is special to all of us. You will forever be "my sunshine." Always one to get up early and kick the covers back, you greeted each day as if to say, "Watch out world, here I come!" I loved that then, and now, I love that you, like me, are a dreamer, visionary, and creator, and that unlike me, you can fly*

on the seat of your pants with the ease and confidence required of a mom with twin boys and a little busy bee like Gracelyn. Those precious grandchildren you have given us are an absolute joy in your mom's and my life.

I will always love your special laugh, wit, and beautiful smile you share with family and friends. In each picture album I leaf through of your growing-up years, your beautiful, bouncy Shirley Temple curls, embody memories that I will always cherish. Your love for God, your friends, and family means everything to us.

I cherish all the great trips we have taken to Florida with you and the kids. The memories we captured with every kind of camera, making handprints at the beach with the kids, remind me that father-time needs to be captured in the here and now, not when I can find the time, but intentionally making time with each other.

We don't often enough get to do what we did recently. I was so happy we had a day together, doing what you wanted, no kids or other family members, just a dad-and-daughter lunch date at your favorite restaurant, relaxing, talking about your life goals, ambitions, and your new home without phone distractions or the need to check social media; just two very intensely purpose-driven people with no agenda taking advantage of a moment to be together as father and daughter.

What a great part of our family story you are to all of us, and you will always remain special to our hearts.

Megan, I couldn't be prouder of you. When you finished your student teaching at Middle Tennessee State University, I was beaming. The fact that you are such an esteemed teacher at Browns Chapel only puffs this father's chest up more. I enjoyed so much coming and watching you teach and read to your class this last year. Your students love you, and I know you love them dearly as well.

I pray God shines His love on you and your family, and may His glorious face brighten and awaken you, His beam of light guide you through every challenging situation, and His bright countenance point you toward a great and lasting future.

Love you darling!

Dad

Kelsey Rae Mauck
August 28, 1991 –

I cannot imagine life without my youngest daughter, Kelsey. Early on, I affectionately dubbed her my "Peanut."

Kelsey was an unexpected gift to us all from heaven. The four of us — Landon, Megan, Raye, and myself — welcomed her home and into the family with open arms. Many times, we would all stand over her bassinet, watching her sleep. I think Landon and Megan felt more like another set of parents at times. They were so cute, making faces in an effort to get Kelsey to smile and laugh, and wanting to help with everything. Kelsey was their baby as much as ours.

As Kelsey grew, she captured our hearts as she tried desperately to outdo her sister in dancing, singing, and special drama presentations they both created for the family.

I remember how close I felt we were to losing her when she was born. An experience like that can make any man an overprotective father, and I've probably leaned that way more often than not when it comes to my Peanut.

Those first twenty-four hours were some of the roughest hours of my life. Due to a low bilirubin count, Kelsey spent her first few hours in the NICU in an incubation unit. It wasn't long before the doctor decided she could be in the main room with the other babies.

On my way out to run a few errands and run by home to pick up a few things Raye needed, I went to admire my baby girl. I immediately noticed Kelsey's breathing seemed slightly labored. I banged on the window until the attendant responded, motioning toward Kelsey and mouthing, "Are you sure she's okay?"

The nurse nodded yes, and I lingered a few moments more while she attended to Kelsey until I was satisfied that everything was indeed okay.

As I walked in the door to our apartment with the list Raye Ann had given me, the phone rang. It was Raye, and she was crying. All I could make out was something was wrong with the baby and the phrase "turned blue." The rest was a blur.

I remember driving fast, running, pacing, and crying out to God to save my baby girl. What seemed like hours turned out to only be about fifteen minutes. When the doctor finally came out and gently put his hand on my shoulder to reassure me, I collapsed in a nearby chair. "Mr Mauck," he said, "take a deep breath. It's going to be alright. Kelsey is going to be just fine."

I stood keeping watch over her incubator for the longest time. I don't remember how long; I just remember I did not want to leave my Peanut.

Kelsey's nickname has shifted from Peanut to KelseyGirl over the years, a name I call her even now at twenty-six years old. Growing up, she was both tomboy and cheerleader, sugar and spice. She loved to play basketball, and I was fortunate to be her coach.

Many underestimated her because of her height (or lack thereof), thinking her too small to even play guard. Her deadly outside shot quickly won them over. Those three pointers helped us win more than a few games. I can assure you, no one overlooks Kelsey now.

Kelsey has an uncanny ability to make people smile, even people she has just met. Her laugh and carefree spirit invite everyone to enjoy the fun. I believe this light heartedness and ability to put people at ease have added to her being one of the premiere nannies in Nashville for several years.

Her knack for getting herself into hilarious situations have left her with many funny stories to share. I'm sure as she enters the University of Tennessee to study speech pathology, she will add many more humorous chapters to her story.

> Kelsey,
>
> Since your first breath, I knew that you would become something very special to us. Without a doubt, your birth was not just a physical one but a love birthed in our hearts. As your father, I now realize you were meant to complete us as a family.
>
> Some of the richest memories of my life are the times in the evenings when your mom would be working her Mary Kay business, and you and I would spend time together. We would do flips with Megan and Landon on the trampoline or ride bikes together. You and I would get on the fastest rides at Kentucky Kingdom, Disney World, and any other theme parks where the family vacationed. We were the crazy ones of the group, and as you grew, you knew how to bait me into doing things none of us should have attempted, like the bungee cord virtual ride that threw us hundreds of feet high in the air and had me screaming at the top of my lungs. I enjoyed every minute of it with you.
>
> Kelsey, there is a serious side to you as well. When you completed your Bachelor's in Elementary Education, you were voted by your peers at Lipscomb as the teacher most likely to succeed

of your entire class. You followed your heart, seeking to become a speech therapist instead, which just proves them right. I'm overwhelmed at your love and care for children with exceptional needs, those experiencing physical challenges, or children with autism and their parents.

I remember one day you thought you had disappointed me and came running down the driveway into my arms...evidence of your tender side. I hope you will always remember my response, "There's nothing in this life you could ever do that would stop me from loving you!"

When you suggested I pick an adventurous place for us for our Dad-and-daughter time this year, I had to one up you and take you to one of highest and fastest zip lines in Tennessee. On our way, we sang, we laughed, we shared funny faces and ended up staying at a bed and breakfast where both of us had beautiful rooms and views from our windows. The food, the ambience, and the mountain atmosphere were so very special and beautiful, weren't they? The zip line's seven different stations and lines were awesome; the fastest one running sixty-five miles per hour over a half mile I think was my favorite. But each one had its own challenges and brand of fun. Watching you do a flip while taking off down the zip line was a highlight for sure.

The water park was amazing as well. I've never ridden a semi-water roller coaster before that day. Above all these things were the pictures we looked at over dinner that night. They weren't just pictures but the imprints planted on my soul. I wasn't just looking at memories captured, but it was seeing my little girl, now a young lady, so beautiful, and hearing you admit you wanted to have a family like ours.

I shared with you my thoughts on how precious life is and that each day needs to count. I tried to keep it light, but you know me, I'm a sentimental man. I remember I tried to lighten things up, jokingly mentioned that I'm there for my parents in their eighties, and someday that might be me and you.

We laughed until you brought it home, saying, "Dad, I will always be there for you just like you have been there for me and your parents."

Kelsey, you have made your mom and me so proud. I know soon you will be married, and we couldn't be happier for you. I will tell you the same thing I told your brother, but will lower the expectations somewhat. We would like, at minimum, a three-seated bobsled with grandkids in it – by year three. Maybe triplets. Twins do run in the family, you know.

Love you!

Dad

The Lost Art of Letters

Back in the old days, instead of movie night or reading a bedtime story, when families gathered at the end of the day, fathers, mothers, or grandparents — the keepers of the story — talked of their younger days. They reminisced about distant relatives, travels, sorrows, and joys passed down from generation to generation. Legacy and heritage came to life through animated storytelling, a once time-honored tradition, filled with personal contact and sacred family moments. It's a lost art I pray will regain prominence in a world where social media has taken over as the cold, impersonal story keeper.

With the fast-paced, technology-infused society we live in, letter writing is also becoming a lost art. Texts, emails, tweets, and Facebook posts all happen in an instant and are as quickly forgotten as soon as the next one comes along. But a letter, intentionally written and delivered, says something to the recipient. It says, "I value you. Giving time to you matters. You matter, and I want you to remember that you do."

When the kids are little, we notch and date their growth on a doorframe somewhere in the house. We log all the firsts, hang the baby pictures and school pictures and make sure family vacations have a photo album. It's easy to find the good, the things to love in the early years.

But when was the last time you put in writing how much you appreciate your tween, teen, or adult children, gave some thought and wrote out what you love about them and shared those things? Have you put your deepest feelings about your children in writing?

For me, letters are the Captain's Log I'm leaving behind, the printed manual of who the people I love are. How much they are loved will guide them through hard times and be a map for doing the same for their loved ones. Tangible vulnerability.

That first round of letters started the tradition. Now, I must admit, I look forward to our Hallmark moment each year. The practice of writing and sharing letters has taught us to be present in the moment, to embrace the vulnerability within a family, and appreciate each other while we can.

I know my children have those tangible pieces of encouragement and love to turn to when I am gone, which will be more important than any company, home, or amount of money I leave.

Charted Steps

Viewing on paper everything a person means to you is sobering and humbling, even therapeutic in a good way. No matter who your family is — a wife and children, extended family or friends — putting your love for them in writing is a gift not only for them but also for you. You're adding to the family story DNA. You're showing the importance of being a keeper of the story.

1. List the people you consider your immediate family and what it is that makes each person unique in the world and special to you. Think back to your first encounter with them. Jot down the highlights in the relationship and try to articulate why those stand out.

2. Take your notes and put them in letter form. This process is not easy or quick. Don't rush through it. Revisit it regularly over a period of weeks. Allow yourself complete freedom to show vulnerability.

3. Pray over each letter as you write it, asking the Lord to give you the words and bring to mind the things He knows each one may need to hear.

4. The big one...once your letters are written, find a time to honor your family and share the letter(s) with them. Don't be disappointed if in the moment, you have a less-than-Hallmark moment as we did. It's the long-term and unspoken impact that's important, the fact that you have left no doubt about who this person is and what they mean to you.

CHAPTER 12

The Wind in Your Sails

> Twenty years from now you will be more disappointed by the things that you didn't do than by the ones you did do. So throw off the bowlines. Sail away from safe harbor. Catch the trade winds in your sails. Explore. Dream. Discover.
>
> — **H. JACKSON BROWN,** PS I LOVE YOU

THE SUN SETS BEAUTIFULLY as I reflect on all I have discovered about my ancestors, contemplate my own family story and my LifeCare journey. More and more I see how connected and interwoven the three have become on this story journey.

While Hans life imprint may have passed over a few generations, what stands out to me is that kingdom purposes are the most powerful of all. My God is a jealous God, and His purposes will not be ignored. How powerful is the God I serve, who reaches down through generations to touch the heart of one and bring them into the kingdom for His purposes? How much more powerful will our life imprints be if we stay focused on His purposes?

Answering the Call

One of my favorite scripture passages is Ecclesiastes 3:1-8:

> "To everything there is a season, and a time to every purpose under the heaven:
> ² A time to be born, and a time to die; a time to plant, and a time to pluck up that which is planted;
> ³ A time to kill, and a time to heal; a time to break down, and a time to build up;
> ⁴ A time to weep, and a time to laugh; a time to mourn, and a time to dance;
> ⁵ A time to cast away stones, and a time to gather stones together; a time to embrace, and a time to refrain from embracing;
> ⁶ A time to get, and a time to lose; a time to keep, and a time to cast away;
> ⁷ A time to rend, and a time to sew; a time to keep silence, and a time to speak;
> ⁸ A time to love, and a time to hate; a time of war, and a time of peace" (KJV).

I love how this passage talks about the seasons of our life. "To everything, there is a season and a time to every purpose under heaven." I hear this as a call from our heavenly Father, reminding us that each season of life is significant enough to be recorded and passed down to our children, the next keepers of the story. It's not just remembering dates, births, deaths, records of marriages, or historical events, but the life that happened around these events, the difficult decisions made, the live-or-die moments, and the struggles. We need to share with our children and grandchildren the humor, the laughter, the tears, the mending of broken relationships found along the way. For me, it's a call to be the keeper of the story.

Friends, there is no better time than now to accept this call and responsibility to be the keeper of the story for your own family. My prayer for you has been one of transformation as you've worked through and journaled the steps to find your own story. This is not a call to just take more family pictures for the sake of having a record, to gather family recipes from moms and aunts, or gather statistics. This is a call for context, for memories, for the back story behind all of these things. It's a call to have conversations, ask questions, record and journal the thoughts and feelings, the sadness and the humor, to capture life in a lasting way, and to make and take the time to share it with friends and family. It's a call to be intentional in creating the life imprint you will leave behind.

Mr. Winchell's Pictures

My first real experience with context surrounding pictures came as a ten-year-old boy. Our neighbor, Mr. Winchell, invited our family over for dinner one night. Afterward, he brought us to the living room where a projector and screen were waiting. He asked if his family could share with us an amazing trip to China that they had taken.

At first, I thought, "Oh, yay. *A slideshow of the family vacation. This is going to be so boring,*" and settled into a comfortable spot ready to daydream about anything else but what was in front of me on the screen.

As the images passed one after the other, Mr. Winchell shared stories. Adventures unfolded. Pictures came to life. The whole Winchell family chimed in, and it made me want to learn more about the Chinese people, culture, and places.

It wasn't the pictures that drew me in and kept my attention; it was the storied context that captured me. I began to feel like I was a part of their party as Dad, Mom, and kids excitedly reminisced about the Great Wall, jumping into paddle boats and almost tipping over, gliding down the river and describing the beautiful scenery, and the lowdown on different kinds of interesting and strange food they ate. Mr. Winchell's presentation made a lasting impression on me, not because of any particular picture, but because of the life in the stories behind each one.

This is the goal of the keeper of the story.

The Least of These

About four years ago, I was invited to lunch at one of our adult daycare centers specializing in rehabilitative handicap services. One of our support staff introduced me to an exceptional young man, nineteen-year-old Willie. I have to admit, even with all of the situations I have witnessed over the years, Willie's physical condition caught me off-guard. Willie had no legs, no arms, nor could he talk. His assistant was in the middle of feeding him, and I asked if it would be better if I came back after he had finished, but both staff members encouraged me to have a seat and even assist with his lunch.

I sat next to Willie trying not to show on my face my feelings of pity and sadness for him. Willie was totally dependent on our staff for all his needs — restroom use, eating, and movement about the facility. He was seat-belted into his wheelchair in several places to keep him from slumping.

I held Willie's cup for him as he drank. When he was finished eating, I stood and stacked his dishes on a tray and turned to set them on another table. All of a sudden, several staff came up to me smiling and pointing at Willie, who was behind me.

"Look, Mr. Mauck, this is what we wanted you to see!"

As I turned around, there was Willie with the most enormous smile I had ever seen in my life. It filled the entire room. Communicating with the only thing he had left, speaking to us in the only language he knew, I was again caught off-guard by the sincerity and genuineness I saw in his smile and his eyes, a smile so contagious, none of us could help but smile just as big right back.

I hugged Willie and left the room quickly, tears filling my eyes as this scripture came to mind, "...Inasmuch as ye have done it unto one of the least of these my brethren, ye have done it unto me" (Matthew 25:40b, KJV).

At that moment, the last two decades flashed through my mind, all the way back to Carlos and me standing on that playground. More than twenty-one years later, it was as if God was smiling back at me, speaking straight to my heart through Willie, peeling back another layer of understanding. My calling wasn't about the millions of dollars managed and thousands of people cared for, but simply being available and loving those He loves as much as He loves me.

Finding My Own Compass

Fully realizing the depth of that love continues to be a lifelong pursuit. Defining moments stand out, such as that day at the care center with Willie, and the night I fully committed my life to Jesus Christ on my dorm room floor at Jackson College of Ministries.

After riding on my parents' coattails of Christianity for so many years, it was refreshing during that hard, questioning season of my life to concentrate on God's Word, focus on music and writing songs, and spend quality time on prayer walks around the grounds. Even so, I was still unsettled and unsure.

That night in my room, though, I knew in my heart, there must be more, more than my parents' faith, more than my college professors' lecture notes, more than the worldly logic and godless worldview I had soaked in during my two years at community college. Deep down, I knew there just had to be clarity and peace and purpose instead of confusion and spiritual turmoil. I had finally come to a place of spiritual and emotional exhaustion and could do nothing but lay on the floor, weep, and wait.

It was there on the floor, after months of searching, studying, praying, and pleading to undeniably feel His presence, to know Him for myself, I heard a reassuring voice say, "Be still, and know that I am God."

I realized He had been with me all along, waiting for me to quiet all the noise I was surrounding myself with and just listen. A peace, an embrace of warmth surrounded me and rushed into the depths of my soul like none I had never known before.

Scriptures and songs that I had learned as a child and in youth group flooded my heart and mind. Tears again flowed as I sang, "Oh, how He loves you and me," and the God of Creation drew me closer and closer.

When I woke the next morning, my confidence in my own faith was absolute. My faith was my own. The clarity of the work Christ did for me on the cross was crystal clear. Nothing I or anyone else could do would ever be good enough to earn a place in heaven. Only by the amazing, selfless sacrifice Jesus made on the cross would I enter into eternity with Him. I knew without a doubt that I was saved by grace through faith.

From that day on, I also knew I would be expected to carry that message to others, not only that He died, but also, and even more importantly, that Jesus rose to conquer death and hell and the grave, that the only way to spend an eternity in heaven is not through our own good works or power, but by the power of the blood of Jesus shed on the cross for us all. There never has been nor will there ever be a greater imprint on my life than that of accepting Jesus as both Savior and Lord of my life.

Route 171

The afternoon of Christmas Day in 2018, I got an unexpected call. My last living aunt, my mother's oldest sister Marcille Hinson, or Aunt Marce as we called her, passed away. After helping Raye Ann clean up the post-Christmas morning chaos, I quickly packed and began the trip south to DeRidder, Louisiana, where my Aunt had lived her entire life, some eighty-eight years.

My plan was to drive all night straight through to DeRidder. After eight hours of nonstop pouring rain and lightning, however, I decided to stop over in Natchez, Mississippi. The storm continued all night.

The next morning, the sun was trying to break through the clouds, and the day seemed brighter. I grabbed a quick breakfast and hit the road. The streets were still wet, and in some places, overrun by runoff from the night's relentless rain.

I didn't really need my GPS, but I went ahead and entered DeRidder into it anyway. I knew the way. I'd been there dozens of times straight across and down through Alexandria, Leesville, and then onto my final destination.

Expecting my old familiar route to pop up, I was surprised when a much longer, unfamiliar one appeared. I tried again. Still not my usual route. A third attempt brought the same result. I realized the flash flooding in the area must be worse than I thought.

So, I took the less-traveled road, heading southwest about forty-five miles out of my way. I listened to all the great, old road-trip-worthy pop songs and Christian radio on Sirius XM.

I thought about my Aunt Marce's life, trying to figure out exactly what I was going to say at the service. What should I talk about? What stories should I tell? Aunt Marce had been such a great influence in my life.

Narrowing down the list of options seemed daunting. Should I talk about how I admired the way she navigated being single? At about the age of twenty, she married a man who unfortunately was not only an alcoholic but also unfaithful. After that relationship ended, she remained single almost thirty years before meeting and marrying a widower named Eddie Lee Hinson. They celebrated twenty-five years together before Eddie passed away.

In counseling others going through loss, transition, and change, I would often refer to Aunt Marce as someone who believed that finding true love should never be determined on a timeline. It was worth the effort to find the right person, no matter how long the wait. Or should I talk about her example of what being a good sibling really meant? Maybe I should talk about how she lived with a kingdom mindset, or maybe the intentionality of her life — always finding ways to serve or be of help to others.

My GPS rerouting again snapped me out of my thoughts, and I started to be concerned about just how far out of the way it was taking me. So, I called my mom and dad and asked what the best route would be to get to DeRidder from where I was. Immediately, both my parents said it was a straight shot due north. I should look for State Route 171 and take it to DeRidder. For some reason, I felt like I had heard of that road before. So, I asked my parents if there was any significance to it.

Laughing, my dad said, "More than any other road you will travel, Kenny."

Well, that intrigued me.

Then I started putting the pieces together. "Is this the same road that leads to Lake Charles, where I was born?" I asked.

In unison, my parents answered, "Yes, the same one."

Dad continued, "Your mom and I drove down 171 when we eloped, and Lake Charles is where your mom and I lived our first year of marriage. Your Pa Paw, Ma Maw, and Aunt Marce came down 171 to see our firstborn child, your sister Candy, in 1956. That's when we finally reconciled with them after leaving DeRidder."

Mom added, "It wasn't until that trip that Ma Maw and Pa Paw finally understood that your dad's first wife was unfaithful and left him for another man. Divorce was not something he wanted. He just wanted to start over."

As I settled into my hotel room in DeRidder that night, I was still trying to piece together my part of the eulogy for Aunt Marce, but my phone call with Mom and Dad kept interrupting my thoughts.

I had grown up with the stories of the singing days of Mom and her sisters — Aunt Marce, Wanda, and Casille. I chuckled as I remembered Mom's childhood nickname. Her sisters called her "Pouchie" instead of Melonee because she was small.

Mom and Dad's elopement and the events surrounding it were family folklore. Slowly, these pieces of family history swirled around me. DeRidder...Route 171...That afternoon along 171, I had driven right by the place of the camp meetings where all of my aunts had accepted Christ. I made a brief stop at the very cemetery in which my Pa Paw and Ma Maw were buried. Next to their graves was the place my Aunt Marce would be laid to rest tomorrow. So much of our family story, spiritual roots, and heritage resided in this place. I went to bed feeling a stirring in my soul, a fresh wind bringing a fresh perspective on my family.

The day of the funeral, I decided to catch one last glimpse of Ma Maw and Pa Paw's house before the service. My heart skipped a beat remembering all the games of tag I had played as a boy in the yard. I closed my eyes and smelled those delicious meals Ma Maw cooked. I saw the big garden out back that Pa Paw had planted to care for his wife, Merta Mae, and their four girls.

Standing in front of the house taking pictures, the whole story flashed before me, not as individual pieces, but like a movie reel: my mom and dad meeting; seeing each other at church; struggling to be together, then trying not to be together; beginning their marriage by running away down Route 171; Ma Maw and Pa Paw coming down 171 to visit when my older sister was born, opening the door for reconciliation. What my parents thought was lost, by grace was found a year later along that same road.

The time pulled me back to reality. I wanted to linger in these memories. I felt God's presence, that He was trying to show me something, but it was as if a veil had not been lifted yet.

However, I didn't want to be late for the service. I was emotionally exhausted from these trips down memory lane, from trying to put my finger on exactly what it was that I was feeling. I was going to need everything I had left just to hold it together and try and give my aunt my best at the service.

What Really Matters

On the way to the church, I thought about my last visit with Aunt Marce. I had walked into the nursing home to see her, dressed up, playing the piano and singing an old-time favorite "I'll Fly Away."

I found an inconspicuous spot behind a pillar, pulled out my phone, and started videoing. Her dementia was acute, and I didn't want to disturb this moment or upset her. After a bit, I put my phone down and walked over to the piano, singing harmony. She finished the song and looked up at me with her smiling, dark-brown eyes and said, "You can sing good harmony." I was a little disappointed. This was one of those times she didn't recognize me.

I smiled back and said, "Thank you. My Aunt Marce and my family taught me how to sing."

Aunt Marce turned fully toward me. "Kenny, is that you?" she asked, laughing and crying at the same time.

"It sure is, Aunt Marce," I replied.

It was an amazing afternoon. We ate lunch together, we laughed, we cried, we reminisced about old times. Before I left, I asked if she would speak with her younger sister, Pouchie. I watched as Mom and her older sister talked on the phone for a few minutes. Then Aunt Marce said, *"Melonee, I just want to go home."*

Pretty much every day since entering the nursing home in Texas years ago, Aunt Marce wanted to go back to her home on Devilla Street in DeRidder. This time, however, she was not referring to that home. She longed for the home she had prayed and sung about her entire life — heaven. She just wanted to be with Jesus.

I looked out at all of the friends and relatives who had gathered to honor my aunt, searching for my next words. The veil was lifting. I saw Hans on the *Samuel*, Frederick on the trail to Ohio, and Samuel on his deathbed.

I felt the pain as Joseph watched his Uncle John walk away for the last time and Wild Bill ignoring the needs of his family. I saw my Great Grandpa Tom's farm and my Grandpa Louie's search for significance. I saw the route that connected us all. I saw the story of my parents held together by Route 171. I saw God's hand of providence through the generations.

I understood what it was He was trying to show me, what it all meant. I did my best to control my emotions, but my voice broke as I concluded, "My Aunt Marce used to take me to the cemetery, to the graves of our relatives, to honor the faithful saints of God and our family. I often wondered why, but today, here in DeRidder, standing up here, I finally get it.

"I stood by a freshly dug grave yesterday, knowing today I would share in honoring her memory, but not sure how I would do that. Today I realize that my GPS taking me out of my way and coming in via State Route 171 was no mistake. God had it all planned out a long time ago. In fact, He has a time and place for each of us.

"I took the less-traveled road to get to DeRidder, Louisiana, but I see now it's made all the difference in my life. Right here in this little town along Route 171, seeing the church where she was raised, the graveyard where we will soon honor her one last time, it's here I'm reminded of the things in life that really matter."

As I headed back toward Nashville, Tennessee, I sang some of the great hymns of old, the favorites of the Nichols' family. I smiled as memories paraded by of Ma Maw and Pa Paw asking us to kneel together for family prayer, thanking the Lord for watching over us another day, and being living examples of the Christian life. The impression of my childhood was not one of the Mauck family in isolation or separation, not one of anger or unforgiveness; the greatest decision my father ever made was marrying one of the Nichols' girls.

The faith of my Ma Maw, Pa Paw, Aunt Marce, and the entire Nichols' family shaped my father, my family, and me. The imprint of faith on my heart and soul passed down to my own children is God's redemption of what could have been a completely different story.

The Greatest Imprint of All

The greatest story and imprint of all time can be found in John 1:1-14, "In the beginning was the Word, and the Word was with God, and the Word was God.... The Word became flesh and made his dwelling among us..." (NIV).

His name is Jesus Christ.

Jesus Christ, the perfect Lamb, the Son of God, came down from His glorious home, lived and walked on this earth, gave His life and paid once and for all the debt owed for sin. His hands and feet were nailed to a cross for our sins. His resurrected spiritual body still carries the imprint of His suffering, His nail-scarred hands as evidence of His love for us. Upon seeing and touching Jesus' hands, even Thomas, the disciple who doubted, proclaimed, "My Lord and my God!"

Friend, this love, this gift is available to all, but it will never be forced on anyone. You have an invitation to be a part of the greatest redemptive story, to have your own story carry the imprint of redemption through the eternal Keeper of the Story, the King of Kings, Lord of Lords, Jesus Christ. He even charged others with the responsibility of becoming the keeper of the story, of chronicling His life-imprinted story for you from four different perspectives in the Gospels of Matthew, Mark, Luke, and John. In fact, the entire Bible is the story of Jesus Christ, His life imprint left for all so that all have the opportunity to hear.

If today you are unsure about where you will spend eternity, I invite you to consider Jesus Christ. There is a hymn, often sang by Mahalia Jackson and George Beverly Shea during Billy Graham Crusades, "Just As I Am," that has become a favorite of mine. I pray these words will bring life to you as they have for me and countless others.

"Just as I am, without one plea,
but that thy blood was shed for me,
and that thou bid'st me come to Thee,
Oh Lamb of God, I come, I come."

The tug you may feel on your heart is not from me. God is calling you to a place of true repentance and freedom. The answer of submission, repentance from sin, and acceptance of the greatest gift ever known can be found in this simple prayer:

God,

I know I have sinned and that my sin separates me from You. I believe Jesus came to this earth, lived, died on the cross, and rose from the grave so that I could be forgiven and live a redeemed story.

Please forgive me. I confess my sins before You knowing the blood of Jesus is washing them away. I know You live today and are calling me now to live for You. I ask You to come into my life and be my Lord and Savior.

Amen

My dear friend, we've come to the end of our journey together. I've done my best to give you everything you need to start recording your own voyage of family, self, and faith discovery.

Leaving your life imprint requires intentionality and purpose. Living purposefully means being present in the moment, catching glimpses of heaven in our everyday life, and sharing them with those you love. It's now up to you to catch the wind in your sails and head for destinations known and unknown, to uncover the themes of love, heartache, joy, searching for significance and redemption that make a story compelling.

Chapter after chapter is just waiting for you to pick up your pen. This priceless treasure, this story of yours and your ancestors', this journey of faith and family once written will live beyond your lifetime and help generations to come live with purpose.

I leave you with one final question...*are you ready to be the keeper of the story?*

* * * * *

Imprints — The Marking of True Inheritance
The Tale of Two Brothers' Tombstones

The graves of two brothers were but four feet apart from each other. One brother was very rich in terms of money and possessions, someone who had listed all his accolades ever accomplished, corporations founded, charities and foundations to which he had given, and a hefty portfolio left in his Last Will and Testament to his children.

His grave was a magnificent monument signified by a beautiful marble tombstone, protected by a golden gate no one could get to or touch. The other brother next to him, though lying in a lovely grave, seemed quite ordinary in comparison. However, his tombstone was open wide with a small bench facing toward his grave, the grass having withered due to a multitude of visitors who took some time to read and stay. Carved by stone on his brother's tombstone were little feet and handprints branded with these embedded words:

> *To all my beloved children, family, and friends, may these imprints recall our walks in the fall, playing hide and seek. You seemed to be growing so tall. Fishing by the lake while holding you and pole.*
>
> *During these gifts of time, I taught you how to eat and live, and yet I hope you learned that there was nothing better than to give. May this seat remind you of things we have done and books we have read.*

*Remember the laughter and tears of shared letters,
happy and sad, but mostly reflecting all the fun we've
had! Best of all, we captured great pictures of all the
memorable things we saw. Oh, the joy of watching
you take risks both large and small, watching love
conquer all your fears. You too will one day dry all your
children's tears.*

*Even though we worked tattered till day's end, watching you help in the garden was all that really mattered.
Yes, I will leave you all my goods and possessions here,
but unfortunately, like sand, the wind will take them
and make them quickly disappear. For there are no
greater riches in life we can share than showing each
other how much we care, like singing to each other or
kneeling during an evening prayer. These are the imprints neither gold nor sliver can buy, like our Savior's
story, no tombstone can hold.*

*With our hands now in His, the Keeper of our redemptive story, we're reminded that heaven is near. So let's
pass this legacy to our little ones now, for these are the
ones who are so longing to hear!*

Mauckism – A True Inherited Imprint
KM

"The greatest tragedy is not to have feared death
throughout one's life, but rather, to come to the end of
life, and realize you never risked living!"

— Kenny Mauck

ABOUT THE AUTHOR

Kenny Mauck is an author, speaker, singer, songwriter, ordained minister, counselor, founder of two faith-based nonprofit organizations, LifeCare Foundations and LifeCare Family Services, and he's the owner of a commercial real estate management company. Kenny received his Master's Degree in Counseling in 1990, from Eastern Michigan University.

He enjoys passionately raising funds for those in need and helping other nonprofits through his new missions organization, LifeStone Springs. This organization provides homes to seniors, support to veterans needing adult day services, and helps an orphanage in the Dominican Republic.

Kenny has been married to his wife, Raye Ann, now for thirty-five years. He is also a proud father of his three endearing adult children, Landon, Megan, and Kelsey. Kenny dearly loves his three grandchildren, twins Easton and Cooper, age eight, and Gracelyn, two years old. He creates and plays treasure hunts with his grandsons in the woods, takes them horseback riding, and plays sports with them. He also enjoys tea parties with his little Gracelyn. All his grandchildren honorably call him "Pop."

His love and passion about living out one's story with purpose is evidenced by living thirty-five miles south of Nashville in the country near a beautiful pastoral setting surrounded by horse farms, a pond, and every outdoor animal imaginable, such as deer, turkeys, ducks, cranes, and geese. He says they give him his early morning wake-up call due to their incessant honking noises.

Kenny has recently resigned after twenty-three years of running his largest nonprofit, which will afford him the opportunity to travel, speak, and share his passion about leaving one's imprinted story as a legacy with those we love, work with, and with whom we have long-lasting friendships.

His love for the outdoors, sports, and music has continued. He still enjoys running, playing gold, touch football, and basketball, riding bikes, rock repelling, hiking, and more recently, flying on a sixty-five mile-per-hour zip line! His love for contemporary jazz and gospel, as well as attending the orchestra in Nashville, exemplifies his love and zest for life.

Kenny's priorities are simplistic: his love for God, family, and friends comes first. Secondly, He enjoys meeting a wide and diverse set of people. You can also meet them on his podcast that's available on YouTube and Facebook and is extremely important to him. In fact, this is one of the ways he expresses his love for Christ and His amazing grace on his life as evidenced in the final chapter of *Leaving Your Life Imprint*. Here, he summarizes that we all are in need of a redemptive story, and Jesus is the only one who can provide that.

This Bible represents God speaking and branding my soul with His hand of favor and direction. Deuteronomy 11:18 says, "Imprint these words of mine on your hearts and minds, bind them as a sign on your hands, and let them be a symbol on your foreheads."

CONTACT INFORMATION & WAYS TO GIVE

Please contact Kenny Mauck via e-mail should you desire to invite him to be an inspirational speaker for your business conferences, nonprofit fundraisers, government events, universities, churches, or community gatherings.

You can also contact Kenny directly at kenny.mauck@lifecarefoundations.org.

When seeking to order a book (s) with or without a tax donation, contact our LifeStone Springs representative at 615-836-8301. A tax-exempt gift letter from LifeStone Springs will be sent to you should you need a receipt. Simply write on your check memo whether your donation is for our LifeCare Foundations, our 24-7 senior and adolescent independent living homes, or the children's orphanage and/or after-school program in La Pressa in the Dominican Republic. A suggested minimum donation of $20.00 or more will prompt us to send you a book, *Leaving Your Life Imprint*, to your home or as a gift to a loved one. (Postage and handling fee will be covered under the donation.) Individuals will also be able purchase the book online through Amazon.com as well.

Should you desire to volunteer, let us know that as well. Kenny's new website and Facebook page is coming soon. New products will allow us to keep supporting our efforts toward these worthy causes. Both our housing and adult daycare services need support as well.

Kenny believes these tax-exempt opportunities will help raise the much-needed support to assist our missionary objectives within the Dominican Republic and in America. Kenny hopes this book will raise awareness for these very worthy causes.

Also, be sure to visit Kenny Mauck's podcast and interviews with other phenomenal legacy speakers, writers, and artists who are available on YouTube and Facebook, as well as us keeping you informed as to Kenny's projects and/or schedule this year.

Our family believes in leaving our life imprints — "handing off" our legacy stories to future generations.

I love to play hide-and-seek with my twin grandsons. Life is not all about meeting goals, but rather living in the moment and having fun with loved ones.

Manny, our dog, has been a constant companion to me throughout the writing of this book.